Adult
Friendship

**SAGE SERIES ON
CLOSE RELATIONSHIPS**

Series Editors
Clyde Hendrick, Ph.D., and
Susan S. Hendrick, Ph.D.

Adult *Friendship*

Rosemary Blieszner
Rebecca G. Adams

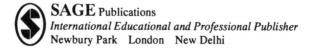

SAGE Publications
International Educational and Professional Publisher
Newbury Park   London   New Delhi

For information address:

SAGE Publications, Inc.
2455 Teller Road
Newbury Park, California 91320

SAGE Publications Ltd.
6 Bonhill Street
London EC2A 4PU
United Kingdom

SAGE Publications India Pvt. Ltd.
M-32 Market
Greater Kailash I
New Delhi 110 048 India

Printed in the United States of America

Library of Congress Cataloging-in-Publication Data

Blieszner, Rosemary.
    Adult friendship / Rosemary Blieszner, Rebecca G. Adams.
        p.   cm.   —(Sage series on close friendships)
    Includes bibliographical references and index.
    ISBN 0-8039-3672-9 (cl). — ISBN 0-8039-3673-7 (pb)
    1. Friendship—United States—Sociological aspects. 2. Adulthood—United States. I. Adams, Rebecca G. II. Title. III. Series.
HM132.5.B55 1992
302.3'4—dc20   92-10088

92 93 94 95 10 9 8 7 6 5 4 3 2 1

Sage Production Editor: Diane S. Foster

Contents

Series Editors' Introduction

When we first began our work on love attitudes more than a decade ago, we did not know what to call our research area. In some ways it represented an extension of earlier work in interpersonal attraction. Most of our scholarly models were psychologists (though sociologists had long been deeply involved in the areas of courtship and marriage), yet we sometimes felt as if our work had no professional "home." That has all changed. Our research not only has a home, it has an extended family as well, and the family is composed of relationship researchers. During the past decade the discipline of close relationships (also called personal relationships and intimate relationships) has emerged, developed, and flourished.

Two aspects of close relationships research should be noted. The first is its rapid growth, resulting in numerous books, journals, handbooks, book series, and professional organizations; but as fast as the field grows, the demand for even more research and knowledge

seems to be ever increasing. Questions about close, personal relationships still far exceed answers. The second noteworthy aspect of
the new discipline of close relationships is its interdisciplinary
nature. The field owes its vitality to scholars from communications,
family studies and human development, psychology (clinical, counseling, developmental, social), and sociology as well as other disciplines such as nursing and social work. It is this interdisciplinary
wellspring that gives close relationships research its diversity and
richness, qualities that we hope to achieve in the current series.

The Sage Series on Close Relationships is designed to acquaint
diverse readers with the most up-to-date information about various
topics in close relationships theory and research. Each volume in the
series covers a particular topic or theme in one area of close relationships. Each book reviews the particular topic area, describes contemporary research in the area (including the authors' own work,
where appropriate), and offers some suggestions for interesting research questions and/or real-world applications related to the topic.
The volumes are designed to be appropriate for students and pro-
fessionals in communication, family studies, psychology, sociology,
and social work, among others. A basic assumption of the series is
that the broad panorama of close relationships can best be protrayed
by authors from multiple disciplines, so that the series cannot be
"captured" by any single disciplinary bias.

The current volume, *Adult Friendship*, explores a topic relevant to
everyone—friendship. Rosemary Blieszner and Rebecca Adams have
reviewed their own research and that of many other scholars in a
book that gives the state-of-the-art on friendship research and pres-
ents a new and integrative model of friendship. The book is clearly
written, yet very scholarly, and packs a tremendous amount of information into a modest number of pages. The authors present a
thoughtful statement about what we know and have yet to learn
concerning adults' friendships. Indeed, lovers may come and go, but
our friends may be with us for life.

Clyde Hendrick
Susan S. Hendrick
Series Editors

Preface

The invitation to contribute a volume on adult friendship for the Sage Series on Close Relationships came at an opportune time. We had recently completed co-editing *Older Adult Friendship: Structure and Process* (Adams & Blieszner, Sage Publications, 1989), which made us aware of the need for a conceptual model of friendship that integrated psychological and sociological constructs. Writing the new book enabled us to develop such a model, clarify the linkages among its elements, use gender as an example of a key individual characteristic in this framework, organize the widely scattered literature on adult friendship, and develop research based on the model.

Because the earlier volume listed Adams as first author, this one names Blieszner first, but we wish to emphasize that our respective contributions to this book were equal. Adams took the lead in developing the model described in Chapter 1, drawing on her structural orientation and relying on Blieszner to develop the process and phase aspects of the model. Blieszner drafted Chapter 2, with input on structural and network analysis from Adams. Adams wrote Chapter 3 and Blieszner wrote Chapters 4 and 5 with editorial comments from the other author. Finally, Adams conceptualized and drafted Chapter 6, to which Blieszner contributed sections on individual, dyadic, network, and society-level interventions.

We thank our colleagues who provided support and assistance with this project. First we acknowledge series editors Susan and Clyde Hendrick, who supplied patient encouragement and helpful editing. We appreciate the advice we received from Daniel Perlman, who read and commented on the entire first draft. We thank Jay A. Mancini, Head of Family and Child Development at Virginia Polytechnic Institute and State University, and Paula Duprey, Julie Peterson, and Carol Pfaffly, graduate research assistants. We also thank William Knox, Head of Sociology at the University of North Carolina at Greensboro, and Glen Godwin and David Yates, graduate assistants. Other colleagues were helpful as well: Scott Johnson reviewed Chapter 6; Paul Luebke, David Mitchell, and David Pratto commented on Figure 1.1; Gordon Bennett, Jerald Leimenstoll, Hyman Rodman, Virginia Stephens, and Robert Wineberg directed us to applied literatures; Jackie Rives and Joan Roach provided secretarial assistance. Alyce Wimbish of Phoenix Graphics, Greensboro, produced the figures. Adams was supported by a UNCG Excellence Foundation Research Grant during the summer of 1991.

With the completion of this project, we continue to celebrate our friendship and look forward to joint research enterprises in the future. We dedicate this book to our youngest best friends, Suzanne, Mark, and Hadley.

ROSEMARY BLIESZNER
REBECCA G. ADAMS

1

An Integrative Model of Friendship

What does friendship mean to you? If you were to ask that question of a group of people, you would receive almost as many answers as there were people in the group. Oh, of course, you would be able to categorize the responses (see Chapter 4). Sharing, caring, helping, and the permanence of the relationship would be mentioned. You would also be able to discern patterns in your "data." The men would tend to mention the importance of doing things with their friends, and the women would remark on the value of intimacy. Young children would mention sharing toys, and older adults would refer to shared life experiences. Rather than the loose clustering of responses and these patterns, however, the tremendous variation in emphasis across individuals would be most obvious.

Why is there such a lack of agreement on the definition of friendship? If you were to ask the same group of people to define relative or neighbor, there would be almost total consensus. Relatives are determined by ties of blood or marriage and neighbors by residence. In other words, these types of relationships are structurally defined. Furthermore, they are institutionalized. Families gather at holidays to affirm their solidarity, and neighbors form associations and have parties to assert their connections. Families and neighborhoods have names. In some societies friendships are also institutionalized. For example, in rural Thai society special friendships are formally initiated by a swearing ritual in which the two participants pledge mutual devotion and unconditional loyalty. Sacred power may be invoked whenever a party violates the vows (Piker, 1968). In contrast, in our society friendship is a voluntary relationship and is not institutionalized (Allan & Adams, 1989; Cohen, 1961; Keller, 1968; Mogey, 1956; Suttles, 1970; Tonnies, 1940; Wiseman, 1986). Friendship is not celebrated formally. We are free to define friendship as we prefer and to be friends with whomever we desire.

Or are we? If friendship is voluntary, why do people choose friends of the same sex, age, race, religion, geographic area, and status levels (Blau, 1973; Booth & Hess, 1974; Laumann, 1973)? If friendship is not institutionalized, how do we know when we are being a good friend? Allan (1989; Allan & Adams, 1989) recently reminded us that freedom regarding friendship in societies such as ours is not as great as it initially appears. Norms exist for whom we choose as friends, how we treat them, and what is acceptable to expect of them. Although friendships in our society are not as structured or as institutionalized as other types of social relationships, they are not entirely voluntary.

Friendship is thus very interesting and complicated to study. Scholars who view friendship as voluntary often emphasize the way personality—disposition—affects friendship. In contrast, scholars with a more sociological perspective emphasize the effects of social structure on friendship, influences that are outside the realm of individual control. Integrating these perspectives in friendship research offers an opportunity to study the effects of personality disposition and social structure simultaneously.

This opportunity is timely. Although friendship is conceptually different from neighbor and kin relationships, these distinctions are becoming less empirically obvious (Adams, 1983). Even though the amount of geographic mobility has remained constant over the past century, long-distance moves have become more common (Parish, 1973). People are more likely to be divorced and less likely to live in close proximity to their families of origin and procreation today than in the past. As Simmel (1955) noted:

> this type of development tends to enlarge the sphere of freedom: not because the affiliation with, and the dependence on groups has been abandoned, but because it has become a matter of choice with whom one affiliates and upon whom one is dependent. (p. 130)

People have more freedom than ever in choosing their neighborhoods and in determining the quality of their family relationships. Rather than making it less important to study friendship as a distinct type of social relationship, this tendency toward greater choice makes it more important. In studying friendship, one focuses on the most voluntary and least institutionalized of all social relationships. To understand how choice and constraint interact in friendship contributes to understanding how they operate in other, increasingly voluntary types of relationships.

Most friendship research has been conducted in the last 20 or 25 years. When Hess (1972) published her classic essay on friendship in *Aging and Society,* only a few theoretical discussions and empirical studies had been reported in the scholarly literature. Although the number and quality of studies on this topic are increasing, there is not really a coherent friendship literature for researchers to read, cite, and develop. Many conceptual and methodological issues thus have remained unresolved (Adams, 1989).

It is time to pause and assess what we know about adult friendship and what we do not know. In other words, it is time to synthesize the research theoretically, identify gaps in the literature, scrutinize the methodologies used, and produce a map for future research. This is the purpose of this volume.

❧ A Model of Friendship

Figure 1.1 depicts a theoretical framework that incorporates both sociological and psychological perspectives on friendship. In the rest of the book this model is used as a framework for synthesizing and criticizing the existing friendship literature, discussing possible applications of findings, and suggesting future research directions. The elements of this model and the connections among them are described in detail following a brief overview.

Age (Figure 1.1, left panel) and other *social and individual characteristics* (middle panel) influence *friendship patterns* (right panel). Age is a proxy measure for *stage of the life course* and *stage of development,* which both affect one another. The effects of other individual characteristics, such as *gender* (or race, class, and so on), are conceptualized both in structural terms, as determining *opportunities for and constraints on friendship,* and in psychological terms, as predicting *personality traits and dispositions.* Stage of life course affects social structural opportunities for and constraints on friendship, and stage of development affects psychological disposition. The forms that the elements of this model take and the relationships among them vary by *structural, cultural, and historical context* (the constellation of symbols, norms, values, beliefs, and fairly permanent social patterns in a society or subgroup of it).

❧ Friendship Patterns

Friendship patterns consist of the *structure* (the form of the ties linking an individual's friends such as the hierarchy and solidarity among them, the similarity of their social positions, the number of friends, the proportion of them who know one another, and the pattern of connections among them), *processes* (the thoughts, feelings, and behaviors involved in acting as friends), and *phases* (the formation, maintenance, and dissolution of friendship networks and of the friendships within them). (See Figure 1.1, right panel.) Structure, processes, and phases influence one another as do the characteristics of *dyads* and *networks.*

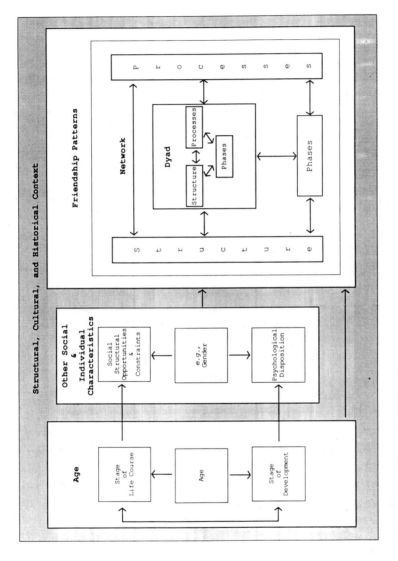

Figure 1.1. Theoretical Model

5

Friendship Structure

Dyadic structure. McWilliams and Blumstein (1991) identified three
major structural aspects of dyadic relationships: *power hierarchy, status
hierarchy,* and *solidarity.* An additional structural aspect of dyadic
relationships is *homogeneity.* Figure 1.2 graphically depicts these dimensions of dyadic friendship structure.

The power and status hierarchies are the vertical dimensions of
relationships, the people's relative positions on power and status.
Weber (1947) stated that power is the "probability that one actor
within a social relationship will be in a position to carry out [her or]
his own will despite resistance" from another (p. 152). Status reflects
the distance between actors in terms of stature, prestige, or moral
worth (Brown, 1965; Goffman, 1971; McWilliams & Blumstein, 1991).
In Figure 1.2 both hierarchical dimensions of friendship are illustrated by the relative placement of the two friends on the staircase.
In examples A and B, the friends are equal, and in examples C and
D, one friend has more status or power than the other.

Figure 1.2 is somewhat misleading because it depicts only one
vertical hierarchy, implying that a partner with relatively more power
also has relatively more status. As McWilliams and Blumstein (1991)
observed, however, these two vertical dimensions are independent.
In some cases the powerful person has greater stature in the eyes of
the other. In other cases the powerful person does not have greater
stature because the exercise of power may violate norms and make
the powerful partner less desirable.

Solidarity is the horizontal dimension or the degree of intimacy
or closeness between the people involved (Brown, 1965). Some researchers treat intimacy as a process variable rather than as a structural one, but it is a fairly widely used measure of the strength of
social ties and of social distance (Marsden & Campbell, 1984). Thus
in our model we distinguish between solidarity as a structural variable and the behavioral process of expressing affection. In Figure 1.2
the people in relationships high in solidarity are facing one another
(examples A and C), and those in relationships low in solidarity are
not (examples B and D).

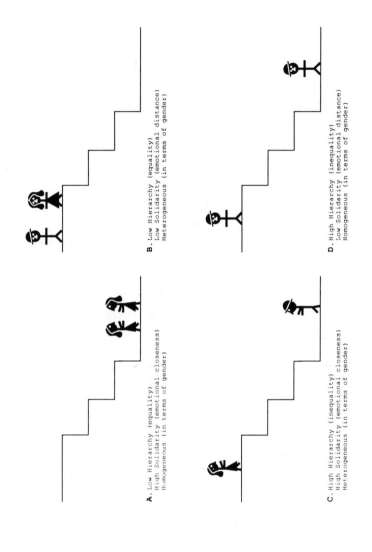

A. Low Hierarchy (equality)
High Solidarity (emotional closeness)
Homogeneous (in terms of gender)

B. Low Hierarchy (equality)
Low Solidarity (emotional distance)
Heterogeneous (in terms of gender)

C. High Hierarchy (inequality)
High Solidarity (emotional closeness)
Heterogeneous (in terms of gender)

D. High Hierarchy (inequality)
Low Solidarity (emotional distance)
Homogeneous (in terms of gender)

Figure 1.2. Examples of Dyadic Structure

Homogeneity is the similarity of the participants in terms of social positions external to the relationship such as gender, race, occupational status, ethnicity, or age. For example, a gender-homogeneous dyad consists of two members of the same sex. Examples A and D depict gender-homogeneous dyads, and examples B and C depict gender-heterogeneous dyads.

Notice that in example C, the female is at the top of stairs and the male is at the bottom. This example reminds us that the internal hierarchy of relationships does not necessarily reflect the relative social positions of the participants in the broader societal context. Although they do not often explicitly state it, researchers seem to assume that the relatively high degrees of homogeneity of the social positions of those who participate in friendship networks indicate the absence of an internal hierarchy. Even in a friendship between two people who occupy similar social positions, one member might have more power or status than the other within the context of their relationship. As Feld and Elmore (1982) suggested, it is important for researchers to investigate the social factors that underlie popularity within particular contexts. In addition, it is important to study the factors that underlie a person's influence over her or his friends. Social position in the world external to the relationship is only one of many possible factors influencing internal hierarchy.

Usually friendships are viewed as intimate, at least to some degree, and egalitarian: dyadic friendships have minimal structure (Allan & Adams, 1989; Thomas, 1987). Many friendship researchers have incorporated this normatively derived definition of friendship into their work a priori, sometimes explicitly, but usually implicitly, by not studying variation on these dimensions. This approach is inadequate. Although using an a priori definition of friendship gives the researcher some degree of confidence that the relationships under study belong in the same category, she or he might end up studying some relationships that participants would not consider as friendship and not studying other relationships that participants would consider as friendship. Furthermore, even widely accepted norms are not necessarily heeded by everyone. Friendship researchers who have included a measure of "degree of intimacy" have found variation on it, even though all of the relationships under study were supposed to be the same. Future research that addresses power or status hierarchy within friendship, rather than a priori excluding hierarchical relationships, could lead to similarly interesting results.

Network structure. The goal of network analysis is the formal representation of the structure of personal relations beyond the dyad (Feger, 1981). Network analysts criticize people who study friendship pairs without considering them in the context of the friendship networks in which they are embedded (Wellman, 1983). Some network researchers analyze population networks—they obtain a description of the myriad ties among all members of a population. Others analyze personal networks—the networks of a set of individuals. The latter approach is most relevant to our model. These researchers have usually been concerned with what affects the characteristics of personal networks and how networks, in turn, affect both the flow of resources to individuals (e.g., emotional support and assistance with instrumental tasks) and individuals' psychological well-being.

Networks have many structural dimensions. In this book we discuss only the basic structural characteristics of friendship networks. In addition to degree of hierarchy, homogeneity, and solidarity, these include the number of participants (*size*), the proportion of all possible friendships that exist among members (*density*), and the patterns of connections among an individual's friends (*configuration*). Figure 1.3 graphically depicts these additional dimensions of structure. The individual is represented by the black dot in the middle, and each friend is represented by a circle.

The most basic structural network variable is size. Size can be measured by simply asking how many friends a respondent has. Researchers who use a strictly structural approach, however, measure size by having the respondent list her or his friends and then counting the number listed. (In Figure 1.3 size of network is thus computed by counting the number of circles.) With the exception of number of friends, in fact, true structural network characteristics are always operationalized with questions about each friendship, subsequently aggregated into network measures (rather than with single global questions about the existence of at least one friendship

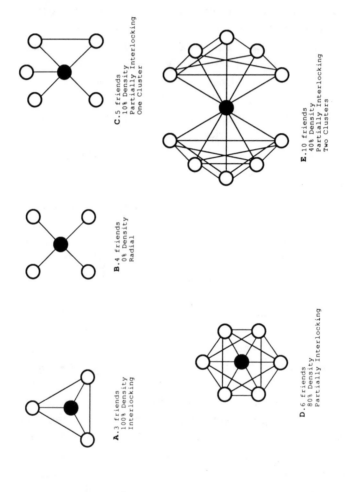

C. 5 friends
10% Density
Partially Interlocking
One Cluster

B. 4 friends
0% Density
Radial

A. 3 friends
100% Density
Interlocking

E. 10 friends
40% Density
Partially Interlocking
Two Clusters

D. 6 friends
80% Density
Partially Interlocking

Figure 1.3. Examples of Network Size, Density, and Configuration

with certain characteristics or about friendship in general). If respondents are not asked to name their friends, it is impossible to measure other structural properties of the relationship. Scholars who use a global measure of size and no aggregate measure of it therefore do not assess other structural measures.

Sometimes researchers interested in the structural properties of relationships adopt a compromise method. They ask a global question about the number of friends and then elicit a list of one or more friends about whom they ask a series of specific questions. The instructions researchers give to respondents about which friends to name vary. For example, some researchers ask the respondents to name their best friend or their three closest friends (e.g., Roberto & Scott, 1986a), others ask them to name two friends from each of multiple levels of emotional closeness (e.g., Blieszner, 1982), and still others ask them to name friends they have met in different contexts (e.g., Fischer, 1982).

As Mitchell (1969) has stated, network density is a measure of "the extent to which links which could exist among persons do in fact exist" (p. 18) and is expressed in terms of a percentage. Most studies of friendship network density use a measure developed by Kephart (1950), modified by Kapferer (1969), and often attributed to Niemeijer (1973). The measure is $100a/[n(n-1)/2]$ where a refers to the total number of links among friends, $[n(n-1)/2]$ refers to the number of potential links among friends, and multiplying by 100 converts the proportion to a percentage. Investigators obtain the data necessary to compute the measure by asking respondents to answer a question about each pair of friends they name. The question varies across studies; a researcher might ask whether they know one another, are friends with one another, or see one another frequently. An affirmative answer constitutes a link. We computed the network densities for the examples in Figure 1.3 using this formula. In example D the individual has 6 friends and 12 links among them. (The links from the individual to friends are not counted.) Density = 100 * 12 / $[6(6-1)/2] = 80\%$.

A concept closely related to network density is network configuration, the pattern of ties within a network (see Feld, 1981; Laumann, 1973; Peretti, 1976; and Salzinger, 1982, for discussions of different ways to characterize network configuration). Some individuals have radial networks, in which none of the friends know one another (Figure 1.3, example B). Other individuals have interlocking networks, in which everyone knows one another (example A). Still others have partially interlocking networks, in which a proportion of the members know one another (examples C, D, and E). In some partially interlocking networks the ties are evenly distributed throughout the network (example D). In others, parts of the network differ in density (examples C and E). In other words, the individual has one or more clusters of friends who know one another but do not know anyone else in the network. Radial networks are 0% dense, interlocking ones are 100% dense, and partially interlocking ones have densities between these extremes. Network configuration, however, can be quite different in two equally dense networks.

Friendship Processes

Friendship processes, reflecting the interactive aspects of friendship patterns, occur between the members of friendship dyads and among members of friendship networks. These processes are the overt behavioral events and the covert cognitive and affective responses that occur when people interact (Kelley, Berscheid, Christensen, Harvey, Huston, Levinger, McClintock, Peplau, & Peterson, 1983). In other words, they are, according to Duck and Sants (1983): "the adverbial properties of interactions" (p. 31).

Dyadic processes. Cognitive processes reflect the internal thoughts that each partner has about herself or himself, the friend, and the friendship. These thoughts concern such things as how one evaluates her or his performance and the partner's performance of the friend role, assesses the stability of the friendship, explains events that occur in the friendship, interprets her or his own behavior as well as the other partner's intentions or needs, and so on. Cognitive processes also include the evaluations and judgments that one person makes of another's attractiveness, character, similarity to the self, and other important qualities. Note that the cognitive process involving perceptions of similarity on psychological attributes such as values, needs, and personality traits is distinct from the structural feature of homogeneity, which refers to similarity of social positions such as gender and age.

Affective processes encompass emotional reactions to friends and friendship. Empathy, trust, loyalty, satisfaction, and commitment to continuing the friendship are all positive or pleasurable emotions. Indifference, anger, hostility, and jealousy are examples of negative or unpleasant emotions that friends may experience. The various affective processes may or may not occur in a given relationship and, if they do, they can vary on the frequency or strength of the feeling (Berscheid, 1983).

Behavioral processes are the action components of friendship. They include communication, such as disclosure of one's thoughts, feelings, and actions. Other behavioral processes are displays of affection, social support or resource exchange, cooperation, accommodation to a friend's desires, joint activities, betrayal, manipulation, conflict, competition, and the like.

The three types of friendship processes interact with each other, such that behaviors can affect thoughts and emotions, cognitive processes can result in affective reactions that in turn influence future actions, and so on. Each friendship process can have a strengthening or a weakening effect on the friendship. Individuals differ both in the extent to which they employ processes strategically versus assuming a more passive stance in the relationship and in the extent to which their dispositions are oriented more toward one type of process than toward others. People either express thoughts, feelings, and actions so their friends are aware of them or keep them hidden from their partners. Moreover, people do not necessarily interact with all friends in their networks in the same manner.

Network processes. The preceding discussion considered friendship processes within one pair of friends. Cognitive, affective, and behavioral processes also occur at the network level, but they operate differently and a wider variety of processes is possible.

As Simmel (Wolff, 1950) observed, relationships involving more than two people differ from dyads. In a dyad the individual is confronted by only one other person. The withdrawal of that one person from the relationship signals its end. People in dyadic relationships are thus dependent on one another, responsible to one another for their actions, and absorbed with one another. In contrast, a relationship involving more than two people is more stable than a dyad because it continues to exist even if one member departs, imposes certain social constraints on its members, and enables individual participants to shift to other members the responsibility for what they have done or not done (see discussion in Coser, 1977).

The cognitive, affective, and behavioral processes discussed above thus operate differently at the network level. For example, a person involved in an isolated dyadic relationship might feel more responsible for helping a friend in need than would a person embedded in a web of friend relationships.

In addition, some processes not possible at the dyadic level can occur. For example, according to Simmel (Coser, 1977), one member of a group might intentionally cause conflict to attain power or other resources, act as a mediator between the disputants, or try to enhance her or his position in the group by sympathizing with one side of the argument.

Proxy measures of processes. So far our discussion of processes has focused on specific thoughts, feelings, and actions that take place between and among friends. Other variables, which we term *proxy measures* of process, have received research attention as well. These include measures of how often and how long processes occur (length of acquaintance, frequency of contact, recency of contact, and average length of each contact). They also include the variety of processes that take place, assessed by multiplexity (number of different activities in which friends participate together) (Jackson, Fischer, & Jones, 1977) and directionality (whether friends behave reciprocally, a particular friend gives more, or that friend receives more) (Cohen & Rajkowski, 1982). These measures of the quantity and variety of interaction do not require much time to assess, which accounts for their popularity in the friendship literature.

We call these variables proxy measures of process because they reveal only *that* interaction takes place but not the *nature* of the processes involved. The underlying assumption of researchers who use these measures exclusively seems to be that a larger quantity and variety of process is better than less. Rather than focusing only on these indirect indicators of friendship interaction, our model also highlights the quality of friendship dynamics directly.

Friendship Phases

Friendships are dynamic relationships that develop and evolve over time. They have beginnings, when partners become acquainted; middles, when solidarity and other features increase, decrease, fluctuate, or remain stable; and, sometimes, endings for any of a variety of reasons. Change from one phase to another—from first impression to closest friendship, for example—can occur slowly or rapidly. The length of each friendship phase—building, sustaining, declining —varies across people and circumstances.

Movement from one friendship phase to another is sometimes deliberate and sometimes occurs by happenstance. Although the language used to describe the trajectory of friendship often implies that friend partners proceed from one phase to another via planned, conscious mechanisms, individuals differ on the extent to which they consciously employ friendship development strategies. Some friendships and changes in them "just happen" without overt effort on the part of either friend.

Dyadic phases. Friendship *formation* involves movement of two people from strangers to acquaintances (or associates; Fischer, 1982) to friends. The beginning phase of friendship involves processes such as identification of or attraction to a potential friend, initial meetings with the potential friend (if a stranger), and getting to know the other and letting the other know oneself.

The *maintenance* phase of friendship is perhaps the most variable period both in terms of the processes that occur and in terms of the degree to which partners consciously attend to the relationship. Friends have many different ways of sustaining their interest in, affection toward, and involvement with each other. From time to time they may consciously or unconsciously evaluate each other, other friendships, friendship opportunities, and relevant social circumstances.

Friends might decide, for example, whether to retain the friendship at its current level of solidarity, change to a higher or lower level of involvement, engage in different activities together, dissolve the friendship, display indifference to it, or carry out a host of other possibilities. The maintenance phase can last for a very long time.

Some friendships enter a *dissolution* phase and others do not. Friendships might endure for decades, with the assumption of indefinite existence; they might end abruptly, as with serious disagreement or the death of one partner; or they might wither to a state of inactivity or out of existence from benign neglect. The causes of friendship dissolution might be involuntary (e.g., death) or voluntary (e.g., disagreement) and external (e.g., relocation) or internal (e.g., lack of support). Processes inherent in the dissolution phase concern the ways that individuals end friendships, ranging from direct and explicit declaration of the parting to more indirect ones such as avoiding the friend or failing to initiate encounters.

Network phases. We can consider friendship phases not only in terms of dyadic interactions, but also with respect to the network. In this case the formation phase involves the emergence of new networks and the integration of individuals and dyads into existing networks. The maintenance phase incorporates the ways that individuals, dyads, and groups sustain the network as it is or change it in some manner. Finally, network dissolution involves the elimination of one person or dyad, elimination of more than one dyad, or breaking up of all the friendship bonds in the network. Researchers have not studied how network processes occur.

Connections Among Elements and Levels of Friendship Patterns

Although researchers have not often examined the connections among the elements and levels of friendship patterns, hypothetically they can influence one another in myriad ways. Each element of friendship patterns—structure, processes, and phases—can affect and be affected by every other element. Similarly, characteristics of the networks and the dyads that compose them can influence one another.

Structure-processes-phases. The structure of friendships constrains and facilitates the processes that occur within them. For example, highly dense networks contribute to friendship stability and to the ease of communication among members. Salzinger (1982) found that members of dense network clusters reported fewer changes in friends over three months than noncluster members, and the changes they did report tended to be gains of cluster members as friends and dissolution of friendships with noncluster members. Adams (1983) reported that elderly women valued dense networks because friends could easily organize themselves during emergencies.

Friendship processes also can alter the structure of relationships. For example, friends who participate in certain activities together might grow closer. Conversely, deception or disputes might dissolve bonds among pairs of individuals or destroy an entire network of friends.

Similarly, friendship structure and phases are intimately connected. For example, as a relationship moves from acquaintanceship to friendship, solidarity increases. If the level of solidarity in an established friendship decreases, the friendship may move toward the dissolution phase.

Friendship development is accomplished through processes, but also, the phase of the friendship affects the interaction that takes place. For example, disclosure is different between acquaintances (initiation phase) than between intimates (maintenance phase), indicating that the outcomes of processes of friendship vary across its phases. In general, the result of processes at the formation phase is either success or lack of success in establishing new friendships; processes during the maintenance phase yield stable, increased, or decreased solidarity; and the aftermath of processes that take place in the dissolution phase is a smaller network of friends.

Dyad-network influence. The characteristics of friendship networks and their member dyads can influence each other in myriad ways. As should be obvious from the preceding discussion, processes at one level can affect structure at another. In addition, network and dyadic structure can affect one another as can network and dyadic processes.

The hierarchy, homogeneity, solidarity, size, and density of friend-ship networks influence and sometimes even constrain the structure of the pairs embedded in them. For example, the density or homo-geneity of a friendship network might reinforce feelings of solidarity within member dyads. The structure of dyads can conversely influ-ence the structure of the overall network, but these effects are prob-ably less likely to occur and are achieved through cognitive, affec-tive, and behavioral processes. For example, the members of dyads with no hierarchy might, through their attitudes, feelings, and be-haviors, create an atmosphere in which network equality was pre-ferred over hierarchy. Of course the more of the constituent dyads that share a given structural characteristic, the more effective their influence would be on network structure.

Cognitive, affective, and behavioral processes of individuals and dyads affect the larger group of friends. Reciprocally, joint activities, group decisions, and shared thoughts, feelings, and opinions of the network as a whole affect the individual members and the bonds among them. Network processes might, for example, affect the sta-bility of friend pairs, the happiness of the partners, or any other aspect of dyadic or individual well-being. The strength of the influence is likely to be a function of the network's structural characteristics.

❧ Friendship and Individual Characteristics

Most researchers who have studied friendship have examined the influence of the characteristics of individuals on friendship pat-terns. Individual characteristics include both social structural posi-tions and psychological dispositions (Figure 1.1, center section).

Effects of Structure and Disposition on Friendship Patterns

Social structure is the pattern of interconnections among social positions whose occupants have access to differing levels of power, prestige, and wealth and thus different opportunities for and con-straints on friendship. Structural effects on friendship include ex-pectations about how friends should act, role demands, and the availability, accessibility, or appropriateness of certain kinds of potential partners.

Dispositional explanations of friendship patterns emphasize the effects of individual characteristics such as personality, motives, and personal preferences (Fischer & Oliker, 1983; Wright, 1989). Some researchers have focused on dispositional differences as the results of socialization, and others have emphasized genetic sources of differentiation (e.g., Rushton, 1989).

In a sense, only a genetic explanation is truly dispositional because people are socialized differently depending on their position in the social structure. The reason for classifying socialization explanations as dispositional is made clearer by considering the difference between what structural and dispositional theorists would suggest to people wanting to change their friendship patterns. A structural theorist would suggest a change of contexts or of social positions. A dispositional theorist would suggest a change in attitudes, personalities, or motives. Whether the old attitudes, personalities, or motives resulted from genes or socialization, it would be the individual disposition that would have to change, not the individual's position in the social structure.

Structuralists have criticized research on the influence of the individuals' characteristics on their friendship patterns for relying mainly on dispositional assumptions and explanations. As Wellman (1983) pointed out, researchers focusing on dispositions assume that people with similar attributes have internalized similar norms and behave in similar ways. This approach ignores the effect of individuals' involvement in structured social relationships. As Allan (1989) observed,

> in much of the literature on friendship, notions like class, age and gender are treated simply as traits that a person has in some form, rather than being regarded as features of the social landscape that facilitate or discourage to differing degrees, in interaction with other aspects of social topography, the emergence of particular social patterns. (p. 34)

But there is a more serious problem with much of this categorical literature: researchers often fail to develop any theoretical argument, be it dispositional or structural, to support their analyses. They simply add variables such as class, religion, race, ethnicity, and gender to their analyses without stating why they think these variables might have important effects. They rarely distinguish, either conceptually or empirically, between the effects on friendship of social structure and psychological disposition. Rather than relying on dispositional explanations to the exclusion of structural ones, as noted in Wellman's (1983) criticism above, the researchers do not develop any theoretical explanation at all.

Effects of Gender on Friendship Patterns

The failure to conceptualize and measure the effects of social structural position and psychological disposition independently is particularly problematic in studies of gender differences. Although we know, for example, that middle-aged men tend to have a larger number of friends and middle-aged women tend to have friendships that are more intimate (Fischer & Oliker, 1983), it is not clear why. It is quite different to say that men have more friends than women because they are more likely to occupy positions that put them in contact with potential friends than to say that men have more friends than women because they are more gregarious. Similarly, it is quite different to attribute the greater intimacy of women's friendships to their better psychological capacity than to their better opportunities to pursue such relationships. *Gender* is often used as a convenient proxy measure for one of these concepts or both. Researchers typically add gender to a set of independent variables predicting friendship patterns without discussing it conceptually and without including measures of the dispositional and structural consequences of it. We therefore know little about the effects of gender on friendship patterns.

A few researchers have presented theoretical justifications for gender differences in friendship patterns. For example, Gillespie, Krannich, and Leffler (1985) offered a structural explanation. They argued that men and women "residing in the same town inhabit socially different communities" (p. 27). Some institutions assumed to serve integrative roles for community members actually work more effectively for men than for women. As a result, patterns of relationships vary for the two genders. Along similar lines, Gerstel (1988) argued that though separated and divorced women are better than men or married women at maintaining old relationships, because of the structure of their lives (the increasing demands on their time and worsened financial situation), they are not very good at developing new ones. The structure of separated and divorced men's lives, on the other hand, provides them with the time and resources to acquire "instant networks" by joining groups composed of people who previously were only acquaintances or strangers (e.g., fraternal organizations, interest groups, or regular patrons of a restaurant or bar).

On the other hand, Fox, Gibbs, and Auerbach (1985) gave a dispositional explanation for gender differences in friendship. The men in their adult sample emphasized instrumental aspects of friendships, and the women emphasized expressive aspects. The authors explained these findings in terms of the "persistence of long-standing cultural norms in gender-differentiated behavior" (p. 499). In other words, women and men are taught to act differently and, as a result, have different friendship styles. Rubin (1985) argued that such explanations of gender differences in friendship patterns, relying on socialization theory, are not adequate. Acknowledging the impact of differential early developmental requirements for boys and girls, Rubin further asserted that unless society ceases to have different expectations of fathers and mothers, men and women will continue to have different types of friendships. Whether ones sees these differences as problematic depends on whether one views certain types of friendship patterns as instrumentally or emotionally more rewarding than others.

ૐ Age and Friendship

Age, another individual level characteristic, is important enough to the model that it warrants separate discussion. Age is used as a proxy measure for both stage of the life course and stage of development (Figure 1.1, left panel). A change from one social position to another (e.g., the transition to motherhood, the process of retirement) signals a change in *stage of the life course*. Age norms govern these transitions. People are aware of the age at which they are supposed to get married, have their first child, retire, and so forth. Although many people deviate from these expectations, a great deal of regularity occurs (Neugarten & Hagestad, 1985).

Stage of development is defined by psychological maturity. For example, Erikson's (1950) theory posits that psychosocial development occurs by resolving challenges emerging from the interaction of person and society, including close relationship interactions. In early adulthood the main issue is learning to establish intimacy. The chief task of middle age is showing concern for the welfare of future generations. In old age individuals must develop a sense of satisfaction with the lives they lived.

Stage of development and stage of the life course both affect one another (double-headed arrow between these two elements in Figure 1.1). A person's level of maturity affects her or his readiness for and likelihood of making role transitions. On the other hand, the roles that people occupy affect their development. For instance, parenthood has effects on one's personality, attitudes, expectations, and so on (Peterson & Rollins, 1987); and being a friend influences one's values, social skills, psychological well-being, and other characteristics (e.g., Smollar & Youniss, 1982).

Effects of Age on Social Structural Opportunities and Constraints and on Disposition

Age affects social structural opportunities and constraints through the mechanism of the life course, and it affects psychological disposition through the mechanism of stage of development (two arrows from the first to the second panel of Figure 1.1). Age is a key basis for allocating people to social positions (Neugarten & Hagestad, 1985). The constellation of social positions determines stage of the life course. For example, someone who is retired, widowed, and has an empty nest is considered old in our society. Each of these social positions has a role—a set of rights and duties or opportunities and constraints—associated with it. In this sense stage of the life course, or the constellation of social positions allocated on the basis of age, influences social structural opportunities and constraints. Not all social positions are allocated on the basis of age; some are allocated, for example, on the basis of gender. Individuals' opportunities and constraints are therefore not totally determined by their stage of the life course.

Besides affecting social structural opportunities and constraints, age also has an impact on psychological disposition. Evidence for stability or change in psychological disposition across stages of development varies according to the theoretical framework employed in the analysis. Research shows, however, that the adult population exhibits a great deal of heterogeneity in both self-concept and personality characteristics. Fiske and Chiriboga (1990) provided evidence to support theories that suggest an interaction between psychological dispositions and the environments that people experience. Thus developmental change can prompt changes in psychological dispositions throughout life.

Effects of Age on Friendship

Many theorists have observed that friendship patterns are likely to change as people make life course transitions (e.g., Allan & Adams, 1989) or as they mature (e.g., Brown, 1991). In practice friendship researchers have rarely distinguished between these two aspects of aging; they use age as a proxy measure for both stage of life course and stage of development. For example, Weiss and Lowenthal (1975) found that older adults, more than middle-aged or younger ones, tended to have complex, multidimensional friendships. Weiss and Lowenthal interpreted the results in light of both differing psychological needs and social norms as people age. Similarly, Stueve and Gerson (1977) asserted that the major influence on friendship networks is the members' positions in the life cycle. Although they interpreted their findings from a life-course perspective, their measure of position in the life cycle (respondent's age combined with the presence and age of children) did not exclude the effects of developmental stage.

❧ Structural, Cultural, and Historical Context

The model should operate differently in different structural, cultural, and historical contexts. *Structure* consists of any fairly permanent pattern such as the stratification of social positions or the way tasks are divided among people in different social positions. *Culture* consists of the shared symbols, beliefs, values, norms, and other agreements of a group such as a society (Babbie, 1988). Structure and culture vary among subgroups of a given society and over *historical time*. The structural, cultural, and historical context affects all of the elements of the model and the relationships among them. It affects the life course stages that are available for people to occupy (Neugarten & Neugarten, 1986), how people mature, the social structural opportunities and constraints and the psychological dispositions associated with various individual and social characteristics such as gender and friendship patterns.

Effects of Structural and
Cultural Context on Friendship

Very little research has been done on friendships outside North America, so it is difficult to compare the model across broad structural and cultural contexts, such as nations. Despite the limited amount of literature, examples of the effect of structural and cultural context on friendship patterns are easy to extract (see Brain, 1976). For example, Jacobson (1968) described the ideology of privileged Africans as supportive of friendship. The opposite of being friendly is being "proud" which is considered abnormal. In contrast, Piker (1968) described rural dwellers of Thailand as being wary of one another and unwilling to undertake binding interpersonal involvement. Allan and Adams (1989) observed a structural difference between the United States and England that affects the friendships of women. In the United States women of all ages belong to a wide range of organizations and, in addition, older women belong to and dominate social centers and clubs catering specifically to the elderly. In Britain, on the other hand, leisure associations for females are rare, both in old age and in earlier life phases. Hall (1989) noted that in the United States friendships develop quickly but only to a relatively superficial level, whereas in Europe friendships take longer to solidify but ultimately tend to be deeper.

Effects of Subcultural Context on Friendship

Structure and culture vary not only by society, but also by *subcultural group* or context within a society. For this reason the model might operate differently among different groups in a given society. For example, different norms and structural constraints impinge on the friendships of college students than on those of nonstudent young adults. Likewise, members of different racial, ethnic, and economic-class groups are subject to varying friendship norms and structural constraints.

Researchers have conducted studies of friendship in a variety of subcultural contexts but have rarely carefully described the structure and processes of relationships. Yet another problem is that very few researchers have used the results of previous subcultural studies to inform their own research, so their findings suggest how one context affects friendship rather than how different characteristics of contexts combine to affect friendship. Because researchers in this tradition have worked in isolation from one another, they have not systematically developed hypotheses to be tested in the future.

A few contextual researchers have carefully outlined the implications of their findings for future studies or have systematically tested hypotheses that could be used in other contexts. For example, Blackbird and Wright (1985; Wright & Blackbird, 1986) examined the effect of status discrepancies on friendships between pastors and parishioners. The hypothesis that friendship is difficult for pastors because they are "put on a pedestal" by their parishioners was derived from ministerial lore. Blackbird and Wright discovered very little support for the pastors' interpretation. Might not one find the same results in a study of the friendships of administrators of another type?

Retsinas and Garrity (1985) also systematically examined and confirmed a series of hypotheses about nursing home residents that could be tested in another context. Residents with strong external ties did not make as many friends within the nursing home as those with weak external ties. In addition status differences (such as gender, age, and ethnicity), so important outside the nursing home, were not as important inside the facility. Similar findings might result from a study of another total institution.

Effects of Historical Context on Friendship

Because empirical research on friendship is a fairly recent phenomenon, the effects of *historical context* on friendship patterns is a virtually unexplored area. Historians have recently begun to examine close relationships of the past, particularly women's friendships in the nineteenth century, using personal documents such as diaries and letters as sources of data (e.g., Smith-Rosenberg, 1975).

At the same time sociologists such as Litwak (1989), Oliker (1989), and Silver (1990) have challenged traditional interpretations of the effects of technological and economic advances on intimate relationships. Traditionally, sociologists believed that intimate relationships deteriorated as industrialization and the modern market economy developed. More recently theorists have argued that commercial society promotes rather than discourages friendships (see Chapter 2).

The historical context also affects psychological dispositions which can, in turn, affect friendship patterns. For example, personality psychologists who study life span development have observed cohort differences in motives and their effect on adult roles (Kogan, 1990). In terms of our model the psychological impact of the historical context would be observed in the extent to which changes over time in the expression of personality dimensions associated with social relationships would affect friendship patterns (see Richardson, 1984). Much theoretical and empirical work needs to be done in history, sociology, psychology, and other disciplines in order to develop a comprehensive understanding of friendship in relation to historical context.

❧ A Preview of the Rest of the Volume

The model of friendship outlined in this chapter was built both by synthesizing the existing empirical literature on friendship and by relying on broader theoretical discussions of social structure, personality, and social interaction. Examining the research findings on friendship in terms of this model makes it possible not only to summarize existing literature, but also to identify areas that need attention. Throughout the rest of this volume we refer to this model as we discuss the structure and process of friendship patterns and the effects of age, gender, and other individual characteristics on them.

In the next chapter we briefly examine changing conceptions of friendship over the course of history. This is followed by an analysis of theoretical and methodological trends that have contributed to the emergence and maturation of research on adult friendship.

The third, fourth, and fifth chapters contain summaries of existing studies and suggestions for future research on the structure, processes, and phases of adult friendship, respectively. We examine and compare what and how much we know about the friendships of young adults, middle-aged people, and older adults and about the influence of gender and the life course on friendship.

In Chapter 6 we address applications of this knowledge. We discuss the possible outcomes of friendship interventions, the levels at which friendship interventions can be implemented, and applied literature that might be useful in designing them.

Our goals for this book are threefold. We aim to show the many interesting and exciting aspects of a key relationship in most peoples' lives, to offer challenges to scholars interested in expanding our understanding about friendship, and to alert practitioners and policymakers to the possible applications of existing and future knowledge about friendship.

2

History of Friendship and Friendship Research

From the days of the ancient Greek and Roman philosophers until now, throughout cultures, friends have been recognized as important sources of affection and enjoyment, understanding and support, companionship and counsel. Scholars have long been concerned with defining friendship and elaborating its functions in individual lives as well as in society as a whole. With the advent of empirical methods in psychology, sociology, and other disciplines came a desire to understand the attributes of friends and friendship. Recent conceptual and methodological advances in the field of social and personal relationships suggest new areas of inquiry, moving toward examination of the structure of friendship patterns, friendship interaction processes, and changes from phase to phase in the development of friendship.

This chapter begins with an overview of various conceptions of friendship throughout history. Then we delineate six trends in the literature that summarize the development and future directions of research on friendship.

ᵶ Historical Conceptions of Friendship

Plato, Aristotle, and Cicero described the qualities of ideal friendship, identified categories and functions of friendship, and analyzed the role of friendship in maintaining a stable society (Brain, 1976; Bukowski, Nappi, & Hoza, 1987). Pakaluck (1991) provided an extensive collection of excerpts from these and other classical thinkers. In general, the earliest theoretical conceptions of friendship were rooted in philosophical questions about the relationship between social justice and personal happiness and in the conviction that wholesome biological and psychological development resulted in spiritual or moral character (Sahakian, 1974). According to Plato, true friendship derived from basic human needs and desires, such as to strive toward goodness, to be affiliated with others, to seek self-understanding, and to love and be loved (Bolotin, 1979; LaBranche, 1975-1976; Price, 1989; Synder & Smith, 1986). Aristotle elaborated on the notion of ideal versus illusory friendship by defining three types of friends, each of which serves different functions. Friendship for the sake of utility and friendship for the sake of pleasure are imperfect forms of friendship because the primary motive is to benefit the person forming the friendship. In contrast, perfect friendship, which benefits both partners, occurs between people who admire each other's qualities of goodness, mutually value the benefits of the friendship, and take pleasure in each other's presence (Bukowski et al., 1987; Synder & Smith, 1986). Cicero's typology of friendship included two forms, a superficial type between dissimilar persons who affiliate for self-beneficial reasons and a deeper type between partners who are similar with respect to character and virtue (Snyder & Smith, 1986).

More recently scholars have had other insights about conceptions of friendship based on consideration of changes in its enactment and functions over historical periods. Lopata (1991) provided one such analysis. From primitive human societies to medieval times people

spent their daily lives in close association not only with their immediate family, but also with many other members of their community.
Presumably they had numerous opportunities to form and nurture
friendships. As commerce developed in medieval Europe, contacts
with friends were mixed with professional meetings, and much social
activity took place in the streets and markets. Friendships existed
across sex, age, and class distinctions, and personal success was tied
to social competence. Gradually, however, the nuclear family placed
more emphasis on privacy, work was separated from the home setting,
and sociability was viewed as incompatible with family life. With
this change friendships became less central and were restricted to
those of similar sex, age, and class. A parallel transformation occurred in America, where early colonial life afforded many opportunities for cross-sex as well as same-sex friendships, but Puritanism
brought restricted social opportunities, especially for women. Later
the progress of industrialization offered little time for leisurely social
contacts, again diminishing the perceived importance of friendship.
Nevertheless, according to Lopata (1991), friend relations in modern society seem to have found a middle ground between those extremes. Spouses are supposed to be friends, employees expect to
find friendly relations at work, and most people place a high value
on friendship despite the pressures of other life domains such as
work and family responsibilities.

Silver (1990) turned to eighteenth-century Scottish Enlightenment
social theorists to examine the roots of contemporary friendship. He
sought to understand the place of friendship in commercial society,
particularly in light of the argument summarized by Lopata (1991)
that the emergence of the market economy led to the demise of intimate relationships outside the family. According to Silver's (1990)
analysis, "commercial society, far from 'contaminating' personal
relations with instrumentalism, [can be seen as] 'purifying' them by
clearly distinguishing friendship from [commercial] interest and
founding friendship on sympathy and affection" (p. 1487). Thus
instead of diminishing in importance, friendship can flourish along
with industrialization because, stated Silver (1990), "only with impersonal markets in products and services does a parallel system of

personal relations emerge whose ethic excludes exchange and utility" (p. 1494).

Litwak (1989) asserted that friendships are, indeed, viable in modern industrialized societies precisely because the unique characteristics of friendships, as compared to kin or neighbor relations for instance, give them special, crucial roles to play in peoples' lives. The fact that friends are chosen and share many aspects of personal characteristics and life-style means that they are well-suited "to provide services that require precise matching of social statuses and values" (p. 85). For instance, because of similarity of age and life-style, friends are often better than anyone else at helping with identity clarification, reminiscing, giving advice, providing socialization, and sharing leisure activities. Primary relationships such as friendships are also more effective than bureaucracies at managing nontechnical tasks. Litwak concluded that people in modern society require a variety of types of friends to meet their needs, and that the constellation of types of friends needed varies over the life course.

In another review of historical perspectives, Oliker (1989) examined gender differences in notions and styles of friendship. She found that the eighteenth- and nineteenth-century patterns described by Lopata (1991) existed more for men than for women. At the same time that men in the marketplace experienced increased emphasis on individualism and decreased emphasis on community, women were engaging in highly romanticized friendships with other women. These friendships, characterized by affection, cooperation, and sociability, provided a counterpoint to the romantic, companionate ideal in marriage that was difficult to acquire in a society that increasingly separated the spheres of men and women (for an extended discussion, see Cate & Lloyd, 1992). Later, though, when romantic friendships were viewed with suspicion, women were encouraged to intensify their emotional involvement in marriage, and their friendships became less romantic in tone. Still, women relied on friendships to provide them support in maintaining their marriages—a function of friendship that endures today. Contrary to what traditional theory predicted, Oliker found that contemporary women's friendships are quite intimate.

✒ The Emergence and Maturation
of Adult Friendship Research

Despite the availability of commentary on friendship in the writings of philosophers and social historians, in modern social relationship research friendship has received relatively little attention from behavioral scientists compared to the attention given to romantic, family, or neighbor relationships. Nevertheless, looking back over the immediate past decades, one can detect a growing interest in studying nonromantic, nonfamily, not necessarily local relationships, and with it, a broadening of the scope and depth of friendship research over the years.

Specifically six trends in friendship research have occurred over the past few decades and have implications for the understanding of adult friendship patterns. They are:

1. expansion of the initial focus on child peer interaction to the study of friendship across the life span
2. movement to study friendship as a distinct category of relationship
3. broadening of adult friendship research from a disciplinary to a multi-disciplinary focus
4. change from studying friendship as a collection of attributes of individuals to studying it as a relationship
5. greater recognition of the importance of studying the *quality* of relationships as well as the *quantity* of interaction
6. expansion of the range of research methods used in friendship studies.

A Lifespan Approach to Friendship

Although ancient philosophers were concerned with manifestations of friendship in adulthood, early empirical research on friendship centered on children, not on adults. Many studies of children's peer relationships and friendships were conducted in the 1920s and 1930s by psychologists, sociologists, and educators. These scientists contributed to the advancement of research methods, including sociometric techniques, observation strategies, and the use of experimental research designs in field settings (Asher & Gottman, 1981). Their studies were adevelopmental, however, typically focusing on one age group but not attempting to examine changes in friendships over time (Renshaw, 1981). In the 1940s, 1950s, and 1960s research on parent-child relationships was more prevalent than that on peer relationships. The Cold War fostered an emphasis on children's cognitive processes and achievement orientation rather than on their social interactions (Rubin & Ross, 1982). The 1970s, though, brought a return of interest in studying children's social skills and peer relationships, including their definitions of friendship, expectations of friendship, and meanings attached to friend interactions (Rubin & Ross, 1982; Selman, 1981). This research also included attention to developmental issues such as the link between childhood social relations and psychological outcomes in adulthood (Rubin & Ross, 1982; Tesch, 1989).

As the emphasis on understanding adolescent development increased, scholars began to recognize both that the nature of friendship was likely to change as youth confronted new developmental tasks and that friends could influence the course of a teenager's development (Tokuno, 1986). Subsequent studies of childhood and adolescent friendship provided theoretical and methodological background for the development of research on adult friendship.

In contrast to the fairly long history of research on child and teenage friendship, systematic study of adult friendship only began in the last 25 years or so. Before that the record shows scattered descriptive studies. For example, Cattell (1934), a psychologist, identified personality and temperament traits associated with being chosen as a friend; Williams (1959) and his students, sociologists, studied the functions of friendship; and Paine (1969), an anthropologist, grappled with distinguishing friendship conceptually from kin and other social relationships. In 1972 Hess published a major review of the friendship studies from the 1940s through the 1960s in which she analyzed the connections among age, life stage, and friendship structure and processes. Her conceptual organization of the literature set the stage for many future studies of friendship.

Although research on the connection between friendship and the structure of the adult life course (see Chapter 3) and on certain friendship processes (see Chapter 4) has a somewhat longer history, most studies of the ways adult friendships are formed and change over time are less than a decade old (see Chapter 5), and there are few investigations of how adult friend relationships contribute to an individual's development (see Blieszner, 1988). Nevertheless, with an increased awareness of the effects of early life experiences on later development, observation of demographic changes leading to the graying of the population, recognition of changes in kinship ties in a mobile society, and shifts in public policy to a greater emphasis on family and other informal supporters for servicing the needs of older adults, gerontologists continue to remind us of the value of studying friendship across the adult years.

Friendship as a Primary Focus

The second movement in friendship research is a transition from treating friendship as indistinct from other types of relationships (e.g., Litwak & Szelenyi, 1969) to investigating it in its own right. In early research on primary relationships the focus was often on marital, kin, and neighbor bonds, with findings related to other types of relationships discussed together as if there were few differences among colleagues, acquaintances, friends, and other nonkin. Based on in-depth questioning specifically about friend relationships (e.g., Adams, 1987; Allan, 1979; Gouldner & Strong, 1987; Matthews, 1986; Oliker, 1989; Rubin, 1985), we now have greater appreciation of the diversity of forms and functions represented by contemporary adult friendships. We also have an understanding of their unique characteristics as well as their similarities to other informal relationships.

Multidisciplinary Perspectives

The third trend reflects a broadening of friendship research from a disciplinary to a multidisciplinary focus. Early philosophical writings about friendship stemmed from concerns about virtue and morality (Bukowski et al., 1987). Anthropologists tended to focus on the cultural functions of friendship as an institution of the social structure. Sociologists traditionally were interested in describing observed patterns of friend interaction but not the processes that gave rise to such patterns (Bell, 1981). Social psychologists studied attitude change, interpersonal processes, and small groups without specific regard to friendship (Sahakian, 1974).

Social scientists now realize that theoretical and applied questions about friendship are often intertwined and cross the boundaries among different disciplines. Thus they have called for research informed by a conjunction of the theoretical perspectives and methods of disciplines such as anthropology, the various counseling fields, education, social and developmental psychology, and sociology (Asher & Gottman, 1981; Bell, 1981; Blieszner, 1989a; Brain, 1976). Also they recognize the importance of studying friendship within its social and cultural context and analyzing cognitive processes and communication strategies used in friendship (Duck & Perlman, 1985).

Friendships as Relationships

Recently the trend has been away from treating friendships as attributes of individuals and toward studying them as relationships. As Wellman (1988) observed, many researchers "treat social structure and process as the sum of individual actors' personal attributes" (p. 31). This traditional and still common approach leads to friendships being "treated as entities individuals possess as individuals" (p. 31). So in the 1950s and 1960s the majority of friendship researchers asked survey questions about such things as the individual's frequency or recency of interaction with friends, or they examined individual differences in the perceived importance of attributes of friends. Although some researchers continue to study friendship in this manner, others have progressed to considering the structure, processes, and phases of friendship dyads and of the networks in which they are embedded.

Network structure. One aspect of studying friendships as relationships involves the investigation of network structure. Wellman (1988) outlined the history of this development, so we need not repeat the details here. He traced the evolution of the perspective from its roots in the substantive questions of British anthropologists (e.g., Barnes, 1954; Bott, 1957) to the American emphasis on quantitative analysis of network form (e.g., Coleman, 1961; Frank, 1981; Moreno, 1934).

Not all network analysts are alike. Wellman (1988) distinguished between formalists, who examine structure to the exclusion of content, and structuralists, who use network analytic concepts to address a wide variety of substantive questions. He also distinguished between those who study networks of entire populations and those who study personal networks. In both cases it is the latter traditions that are most often used by friendship researchers. Laumann (1973) and Fischer (1982) are examples of influential friendship researchers who addressed substantive questions through the use of personal network analytic techniques (see Chapter 3).

Friendship processes and phases. Another aspect of studying friendships as relationships involves looking at dynamic processes and phases of interaction. The publication of Newcomb's *The Acquaintance Process* in 1961 was a landmark in adult friendship research from a process and phase perspective. Newcomb arranged an experimental setting in which male strangers took up residence, then he tracked their progress toward acquaintanceship and friendship over the course of an academic semester at college. He replicated the study in the following academic year. Based on weekly data collections, Newcomb was able to examine questions such as the role of perceived similarity in ratings of attractiveness among the residents, influences on stability or change in attraction over time, and the effects of propinquity on communication, and, hence, on attraction. Newcomb's work was followed by similar short-term longitudinal studies of friendship formation (Altman & Taylor, 1973; Duck & Craig, 1978; Duck & Spencer, 1972; LaGaipa, 1977) and delineations of levels of friendship or stages of friendship development (Coleman, 1977; Levinger & Snoek, 1972). More recently additional short-term longitudinal studies designed to trace the formation and character of friendship over time have appeared in the literature (e.g., Berg, 1984; Hays, 1984, 1985; Shea, Thompson, & Blieszner, 1988).

Research on dynamic aspects of association increased dramatically in the 1980s, as attested by the recent publication of major reviews on processes of close relationships in general (Clark & Reis, 1988; Duck, 1990; Duck & Sants, 1983; Hendrick & Hendrick, 1992; Kelley et al., 1983), as well as on processes of friendship in particular (Chown,

1981; Hays, 1988; Reisman, 1981). A number of friendship processes have been analyzed, including self-disclosure, commitment, attributions, conflict, and changes in closeness over time, as examples. Duck (1990) pointed out, however, that although many researchers acknowledge that relationships are not merely interpersonal states, but rather are the products of ongoing interactions and cognitions, they nevertheless fail to examine the dyadic or relational level of analysis. We note further that although analysis of processes and phases of friendship tends to be located at the dyadic level of interaction, a focus on structural aspects of friendship mainly involves study of networks, another level of relationship analysis that has been neglected in friendship research.

Quality of Friend Relations

The fifth trend in friendship research is recognition of the importance of examining the quality of relationships along with the quantity of interaction. Critics of the state of friendship research (e.g., Adams, 1989; Allan, 1979) have pointed out that one of the most widely used measures of friendship, rate of contact, reveals very little about the content or meaning of the relationship. Similarly, counting the amount or frequency of contact does not convey much about the impact of friendship on a person's well-being (Mancini & Blieszner, 1992). A more productive focus is on understanding the meaning that partners attribute to friendship and factors that contribute to friendship harmony or discord (Roberto, 1989; Rook, 1989). This new direction includes examination of how people define friendship (Adams, 1989), the relationship between the properties of friendship and the personal characteristics of friends (Allan, 1979), and the outcomes of friendship for individuals, dyads, networks, and the larger society (see Chapter 6).

Multiple Research Designs and Methods

Finally, the sixth recent development in friendship research is a broadening of the research methods used to study friendship. Although participant observation studies that included discussion of friendship appeared in the 1950s, 1960s, and 1970s (e.g., Gans, 1962;

Hochschild, 1973; Liebow, 1967; Seeley, Sim, & Loosley, 1956; Whyte, 1956), much research that touched on friendship was based either on laboratory experiments or on surveys. Traditional experimental and survey designs and even observational and structured-question self-report data collection methods all have limitations in what they can reveal about friendship. Thus scholars studying friendship more recently have acknowledged the need to employ, either alone or in conjunction with quantitative techniques, qualitative methods that permit detailed open-ended questioning about friend interactions and the meanings partners ascribe to them (e.g., Adams, 1987; Allan, 1979; Gouldner & Strong, 1987; Matthews, 1986; Oliker, 1989; Rubin, 1985).

Scholars have also begun to use quantitative techniques in ways that enhance friendship research. Based on surveys of older adult friendship in the 1960s to 1980s, Adams (1988) noted a shift toward defining friendship in terms of its characteristics, examining the quality of the content or process of interaction, asking questions about specific friends instead of the more global friendship in general, and using the dyad as the unit of analysis. A caveat is in order, however: Adams noted that a larger percentage of studies using such approaches was conducted by female than by male researchers. This gender bias among authors of different types of studies has important implications for the conclusions one can draw from existing research. Friendships of women versus men may be characterized inaccurately, and gender differences may be exaggerated in some respects and hidden in others, depending on the sex of the researcher. So regardless of the study design, investigators must be careful to include both female and male perspectives and a wide range of questions in their studies.

⁊ Summary

Over the course of history conceptions of friendship have broadened from abstract philosophical treatises about ideal friendship to recognition of the vital role that friends play in providing the social support considered so essential for coping successfully with life's exigencies. Empirical research on adult friendship has emerged and proceeded in recent years along the lines of highlighting friendship as a primary relationship in peoples' lives, beginning to examine both structure and process aspects of friendship and investigating the quality of friendship in addition to the amount of contact. Increasingly, friendship researchers have taken a multidisciplinary perspective on their topic and employed qualitative methods to uncover phenomenological aspects of friendship. We provide a detailed discussion of recent empirical manifestations of these trends in Chapters 3, 4, and 5.

3

The Internal Structure
of Friendship

In Chapter 1 we discussed the components of friendship patterns, including structure, processes, and phases. Chapters 3, 4, and 5 present research on these components. We report the findings by stage of the life course with emphasis on the effects of gender. The differences in friendship patterns across age groups and genders discussed in the next three chapters are subject to the alternative interpretations mentioned in Chapter 1. Age is a proxy measure for both stage of the life course and stage of development. Sometimes age group differences also reflect cohort differences—changes in the way people born and socialized during different periods of history behave and feel. Gender effects can reflect differences in psychological dispositions or in social structural opportunities and constraints. The researchers whose work is summarized in the following three chapters generally did not make these conceptual distinctions when reporting age and gender effects, so the meaning of the findings is not clear. Besides examining age or gender differences, it is also important to note and interpret age and gender similarities. Again researchers have not often assumed such a focus.

Summarizing the literature on friendship patterns is problematic for other reasons as well. First, the division of the life course into stages is not fine enough in most of the friendship literature. In most studies all adults were grouped together and, sometimes, age was not even treated as a variable. It is especially difficult to analyze the friendship patterns of adults between the college years and old age. Second, gender was often not included as a variable even when people of both sexes were sample members. Sometimes the results were reported by gender in tables, but neither was their significance tested nor their importance or meaning discussed. Finally, and perhaps most serious, most investigations of friendship patterns are unique. Each study design consisted of a different combination of definition of friendship, selection of concepts, and measures of concepts. Furthermore, the existing research focused on a hodgepodge of special populations (Adams, 1989). It is thus often impossible to compare findings across studies or to make generalizations.

We discussed many of the measurement issues involved in friendship research in Chapter 1. An additional issue affects the outcome of the measurement of every component of friendship patterns—how friendship is defined for respondents before they are asked to list their friends. Depending on their theoretical or practical purpose, researchers sometimes let the respondents define friendship for themselves or limit the definition of friendship in some way, such as to emotionally close, proximate, frequently seen, nonwork, or nonkin relationships (Adams, 1989). The structure, processes, and phases of a friendship network might be quite different depending on which definition is applied.

The focus of Chapter 3 is the internal structure of friendship patterns. The basic elements of dyadic structure include the relative power and status of the participants (internal hierarchy), the similarity or dissimilarity of the social positions of the participants (homogeneity), and the intimacy binding the participants to one another (solidarity). These are also basic elements of network structure, which additionally include the number of the participants in the friendship network (size), the extent to which the possible connections among them exist (density), and the pattern of these connections (configuration). Although networks have additional structural dimensions, we do not have space to discuss them. Thus in this chapter we review studies on all of the basic aspects of friendship structure, except for internal hierarchy, which has not been researched.

On the other hand, we only review studies of friendship structure in which the researcher asked questions about one or more specific relationships, rather than global questions about friendships in general or questions about the existence of a friend with specific characteristics. (The only exception to this criterion for inclusion is studies in which the researchers asked a global question about the number of friends.) So, for example, even though intimacy and closeness are measures of network solidarity, we do not include studies in which the measures consisted only of questions such as: "About how close would you say you feel to your friends?" or "Do you have a friend in whom you confide?" Keeping in mind the difficulties of reviewing this literature, the resulting necessary compromises of purpose, and the measurement issues discussed here and in Chapter 1, we turn to the literature summary.

❧ College Student Friendships

This section is not titled Young Adult Friendships because the only studies of the friendship structure of young adults uncovered during our bibliographic search were of college or graduate student populations. We therefore know nothing about the friendship structure of young adults who enter the work force, marry, or lack direction after high school.

This selectivity raises a question: How might the structure of college and university students' friendships differ from that of other young adults? Although the composition of the student population varies across colleges and universities, the population of any given institution tends to be fairly homogeneous on the dimensions of class, age, and race. This is especially true of private institutions, which are also more likely than public institutions to be homogeneous in terms of gender. It is thus possible that college student friendships are relatively more homogeneous than those of nonstudent young adults. College students interact mainly with peers, unless they work off campus or live at home. One would thus expect friends to compose a larger proportion of college student social networks than of nonstudent young adult networks. This possibility suggests that college students might have relatively more friends than nonstudent young adults and, because their friends are likely to come from the same institution, a denser friendship network. Because of the greater amount of time that college students spend with peers and the probable homogeneity and density of their networks, one would also expect their friendship networks to be relatively intimate. Of course, if college students are employed, they may have less time for friendship than do their nonstudent age peers.

Knowing about the structure of the friendship networks of college students is thus not the same as knowing about the friendships of young adults in general. Compared to other young adults, college students probably have larger, more homogeneous, denser, and more intimate friendship networks. Nonstudent young adults may, in fact, have networks that resemble those of mature adults more than they resemble those of their age peers enrolled in college.

Size

The mean reported size of the friendship networks of college students varied tremendously by study, possibly because the student populations and measures of size differed. For example, students at a university in Ontario reported an average of 9.1 friends (Wister & Avison, 1982); Chinese-American students reported an average of about 4 (Ting-Toomey, 1981); and graduate and undergraduate students in Pennsylvania reported an average of 2.88 (Johnson & Leslie, 1982).

Research on predictors of the size of college students' networks is more informative. For example, gender is a predictor; female college students have more friends than male college students (Johnson &

Leslie, 1982; Peretti, 1976). Also several researchers demonstrated that the more involved students are in romantic relationships, the fewer friends they have (Fischer, Sollie, Sorrell, & Green, 1989; Johnson & Leslie, 1982; Milardo, 1982). On the other hand, the population density of the community surrounding the university appears to have no effect on the size of friendship networks. Neither Franck (1980), assessing students in New York City and rural New York State, nor Sutcliffe and Crabbe (1963), comparing across inner city, suburban, and rural areas of England, found any significant differences in the average number of friendships.

Homogeneity

Researchers have examined the homogeneity of college student friendship networks in terms of nationality, ethnicity, and gender. The disparate studies have two distinct themes—the effect of homogeneity of context on the homogeneity of networks and the connection between homogeneity and other network characteristics.

The results for the effect of context on network composition are varied. For example, in studies conducted in English dormitories, friendship networks tended to be homogeneous on the dimension of nationality, regardless of the composition of the context (i.e., the mixture of English and foreign students) (Bochner, Hutnik, & Furnham, 1985; Furnham & Alibhai, 1985). In contrast, Ting-Toomey (1981) found that the ethnic composition of the high schools her Chinese-American student subjects had previously attended was correlated with the ethnic composition of their friendship networks.

Peretti (1976, 1977) is one of the few researchers to study the connection between the homogeneity of college students' friendship networks and other characteristics of their networks. Looking at the structure of friendships among students at an almost entirely black Chicago university, Peretti (1977) reported that heterogeneous friendship clusters were smaller than homogeneous ones, probably because of the greater potential intimacy in cross-sex friendships. Peretti (1976) also found gender differences in the configuration of same-sex and opposite-sex friendships. Females were more likely than males to have larger clusters of same-sex friends, but were slightly less likely than males to have large clusters that included opposite-sex friends.

Density and Configuration

Other than Peretti's (1977) work on the connection between network configuration and homogeneity, very little research exists on the density or configuration of the friendship networks of college students. This fact is not surprising because collecting the information necessary to compute density is time consuming and best done in face-to-face interviews rather than via the self-administered questionnaires typically used in studies of college-student populations. Two interesting exceptions illustrate the value of considering the density of networks in addition to the characteristics more frequently studied. Together they demonstrate that friendship network density might possibly affect behavior of the participants and the characteristics of the constituent dyads.

In a study of marijuana use among university students in Ontario, Wister and Avison (1982) reported that the mean friendship network density was 37.9%. In other words, more than one-third of the average student's closest associates were friends with one another. Furthermore, the authors found that marijuana users were most likely to have dense friendship networks in which there was considerable agreement that marijuana use is appropriate in a wide variety of circumstances. This result suggests that conformity of behavior might be greatest among the members of dense networks.

Salzinger's (1982) study is important both because it is one of the few on young adults that included density as a variable and because it is one of the few studies on any age group that examined the connection between friendship network and dyadic characteristics. Unlike other research reviewed in this chapter, in this investigation of white juniors and seniors in Boston, Salzinger studied the overall population network rather than the personal networks of a sample of individuals from the population. The data revealed eight clusters—groups of three or more people who each had at least one friend in common and who had more ties within than outside the group. Salzinger concluded that, compared to loose networks, dense networks are relatively more limiting, stable, and likely to include reciprocally chosen dyads.

Solidarity

Researchers have many techniques for measuring network solidarity. Johnson and Leslie (1982) assessed solidarity in two ways: by asking the respondents (a) how important they considered the opinions of each friend in making decisions about their personal lives, and (b) how much they confided in each of them. Ting-Toomey (1981) asked her respondents how intimate or personal their conversations were with each friend. Sutcliffe and Crabbe (1963) classified each contact named by the respondents as an acquaintance, friend, or best friend, depending on the pattern of responses to 56 items, such as sharing of confidences, likes and interests, and the incidence of criticism, antagonism, and argument. Peretti (1976) measured solidarity by asking 13 questions related to social intimacy, such as "I feel very much at ease and relaxed with my friend" and "My friend and I have common interests based on our common experiences." Barth and Kinder (1988) measured solidarity with Rands and Levinger's (1979) involvement scale on which the respondents rated the likelihood of 23 interactions occurring within a designated relationship.

Each of these studies included at least one predictor of network solidarity. Johnson and Leslie (1982) reported a slight increase in importance of friends and in disclosure to them across stages of romantic involvement with a partner. As relationships proceeded from regular dating to exclusive dating to engagement to marriage, there was a general decline in network solidarity that was particularly large at marriage. In addition, compared to college men, college women disclosed more to friends and considered them more important in making personal decisions. Men and women did not, however, differ in the tendency to withdraw from their friendship networks with increasing romantic involvement.

In a study of undergraduate students in Florida, Barth and Kinder (1988) also reported that college women exhibited higher solidarity with their friends. Specifically they found that female same-sex friendships exhibited greater involvement than male same-sex friendships within each level of friendship (casual, good, and close). Also the sex difference was greater between sex-typed than between androgynous individuals.

Sutcliffe and Crabbe (1963) examined the effect of degree of urbanity on the incidence of best friends. Although the number of best friends varied by the area in which the respondent lived, the number of best friends did not increase from urban to rural areas. In other words, one should not assume that college student friendship networks in rural areas are higher in solidarity than those in urban areas.

Two studies showed that the larger the size of the network, the less solidarity it exhibits (Peretti, 1976; Ting-Toomey, 1981). These authors also discussed the connection between the similarity of network members and solidarity. Peretti reported that a higher proportion of opposite-sex friendships than of same-sex friendships was characterized by high solidarity. Ting-Toomey found that respondents who perceived a high proportion of their friends to be similar to them exhibited more network solidarity than did others.

֎ Adult Friendships

Ideally at this juncture we would discuss the structure of middle-aged adults' friendships. Unfortunately very few studies of friendship structure focused exclusively on this age group or, in studies of multiple age groups, presented results for middle-aged persons separately. Thus we summarize findings on the friendship structure of adults who were older than 17 years old. Some of the studies had samples closely limited to middle-aged persons, and, in most of them, the middle-aged were the dominant group. This research does, however, include nonresidential college students and older adults who did not live in long-term care facilities.

Adults live different lives from those of most college students. They have a greater number of demands and more varied demands on their time. They are more likely to spend a large amount of time with their families and to have full-time jobs. Compared to college students, mature adults would be expected to interact with a wider variety of people and to have less time to socialize with friends. One would thus expect them to have fewer friends and networks characterized by less homogeneity, density, and solidarity.

Size

Although many studies of adult friendship included measures of the size of the network, researchers generally have reported averages by subgroup rather than an overall mean for the general adult population. These averages vary tremendously, not only because of the differences in population, but also because of the differences in the definition of friend.

Fischer (1982) studied the general adult population of several Northern California communities, focusing on associates rather than on friends per se. His respondents named an average of 7.8 nonkin associates, but this is most likely an overestimate of average number of friends. He also reported figures (probably underestimating the average number of friends) on the number of all nonkin associates except for work contacts, members of the same organizations, acquaintances, and neighbors. This average increased with each level of urbanization, from 3.0 in semirural areas to 3.6 in the core of the inner city. The number of actual friends that Fischer's respondents would have reported with a more direct question therefore is between 3.0 and 7.8.

In a study of blue-collar respondents at four different stages of life, Weiss and Lowenthal (1975) reported that the parents of teenagers had an average of 4.7 friends, and people in the preretirement stage had an average of 6.0 friends. Note that these figures are within the range suggested by Fischer's study.

Homogeneity

Adult friendship networks tend to be homogeneous in terms of occupational status, ethnicity, age, marital status, income, education, gender, and religion (e.g., Fischer, 1982; Jackson, 1977; Laumann, 1973; Verbrugge, 1977). Researchers have repeatedly found that higher-status adults have more homogeneous networks (Jackson, 1977; Laumann, 1973; Schutte & Light, 1978). Verbrugge (1977) observed that when people chose friends of dissimilar status, they tended to choose friends of higher status than themselves. Therefore people in the highest status categories (e.g., in terms of education, age, and occupational prestige) tended to have homogeneous networks. In contrast to this overall pattern, Laumann (1973) reported that Catholics had networks more homogeneous in terms of ethnicity and religion than did Protestants, and Jackson (1977) found that men working for the state or in production jobs had more homogeneous networks than men in other types of jobs.

Most of the literature on homogeneity assumes that people have networks consisting predominantly of status-similars because they voluntarily choose them. Choice definitely contributes to homogeneity (McPherson & Smith-Lovin, 1987), but Fischer (1982) and Feld (1982) both forcefully reminded us that the context in which friendships are formed affects network composition as well. In generalizing from an analysis of his Northern California data, Fischer observed that urban residence increases access to all types of people. For adults of majority status (i.e., a common status such as married), the prevalence of status-dissimilars was most important, but for people of minority status (i.e., a less common status such as the never married), the availability of status-similars was most important. In other words, in cities compared to less urban areas, majority people had more heterogeneous networks and minority people had more homogeneous networks.

In a reanalysis of Fischer's data, Feld (1982) concluded that most relationships originate in activities that bring together homogeneous groups of people. The more homogeneous these sets of people are, the more homogeneous are the resulting friendship networks. McPherson and Smith-Lovin (1987) confirmed Feld's conclusions with data from 10 communities in Nebraska, but they also demonstrated that similar-status choices made within the group context contributed to homogeneity as well. Jackson (1977) observed that the homogeneity of the networks themselves is reinforcing. Once adults have homogeneous networks, they are more likely to recruit new friends similar to themselves and their friends.

Density and Configuration

The Detroit Area Study and the Northern California Study included different measures of network density. In the Detroit Area Study the interviewers asked about the existence of friendship connections among the respondents' three closest friends (Laumann, 1973). In the Northern California Study respondents listed five persons in response to a series of questions about who cared for their home, visited or went out with them socially, discussed hobbies or personal matters with them, gave them advice, or loaned them money. Then the interviewer asked whether each pair of associates knew one another well (Fischer, 1982).

Laumann (1973) found that 27% of his respondents had networks that were completely interlocking (100% dense). Remember, this rather high percentage results from his measurement of the density of the network defined as only the three closest friends. An additional 42% had partially interlocking networks, and 31% had radial networks (0% density). Fischer (1982) reported that the average density of the network of associates was 44% and that the more relatives and the fewer nonrelatives in the network, the denser it was. This suggests that friendship network density would have been lower.

Network density varied systematically by individual characteristics. Fischer (1982) found that the networks of the associates of less-affluent and less-educated adults tended to be denser, as did those of residents who had lived in their area for a long time and those of people living in less urban areas. Laumann (1973) examined the relationship between network density and age, number of paternal generations in the United States, religious preference, ethnic group, educational attainment, occupation, and proportion of life spent in Detroit. Only religious preference was correlated with density; Catholics and Jews had denser networks than other male adults.

Bibliographic research revealed only one study of the connection between the characteristics of the context and network density. In a reanalysis of the Detroit Area data Baldassare (1977) reported that, contrary to what he had expected, the population density of census tracts was not related to the density of friendship networks.

Researchers have also examined the connection between density and other network characteristics. In a reanalysis of the Northern California data Feld (1981) reported that network density was positively related to the average solidarity of the networks. Jackson et al. (1977) found the same results in their reanalysis of the Detroit Area Study data. In addition, they noted that network density was not related to age homogeneity or occupational homogeneity. Analyzing the same data set, Laumann (1973) reported that density was positively related to ethnoreligious homogeneity and number of close friends.

Solidarity

Most of the research on network solidarity concerned its connection to other network characteristics and thus was discussed in previous subsections. The only link that has been firmly established is between solidarity and density (Feld, 1981; Jackson et al., 1977).

❧ Old Age Friendships

Failing health, retirement, widowhood, and relocation modify the opportunities for some aging people to make and maintain friendships (Allan & Adams, 1989). Some of these changes signify a decrease in opportunities for friendship, and others signify an increase. Together both types of changes create a different context for later-life friendship than for middle-aged friendship. With the possible exception of widowhood, these changes make the immediate environment more important to the friendships of older adults than to the friendships of those at earlier stages of life. Failing health limits mobility. Retirement eliminates one source of everyday interaction with friends, making the neighborhood a relatively more important source. Relocation means new local friendships have to be established. Because of these changes, compared to friendships of middle-aged persons, one would expect the local friendship networks of older adults to be smaller (because they might find few compatible companions close to home), more homogeneous (because neighborhoods tend to attract similar people), denser (because people who live in the same place are likely to know one another), and higher in solidarity (because people who interact frequently with one another are likely to grow close). Of course, however, all friendships are not local (Adams, 1985-1986), and thus predicting the overall structure of the friendship network of older adults is complicated.

The populations of young adults and old people have something in common. Some members of each group live in age-segregated environments. As mentioned earlier, researchers have not studied the friendship structure of young adults who do not go to school. Although most of the studies of older adults are of people living in age-integrated contexts, a few studies of the friendship structure of older adults living in age-segregated housing and in long-term care facilities exist. One would expect the structure of the friendship networks of older adults living in age-integrated environments to be similar to that of middle-aged adults' networks, because such elderly people are unlikely to have experienced changes in circumstances.

Size

The findings on the size of older adults' friendship networks were inconsistent across studies, probably because the samples of the older population and the measures used to assess network size differed. The only general population for which researchers have reported the size of friendship networks is people from four small towns in Missouri; the respondents claimed an average of six friends (Pihlblad & Adams, 1972). Researchers observed nursing home residents interacting with a median of one friend and a maximum of six (Retsinas & Garrity, 1985).

Many studies reporting on the size of friendship network are exclusively of female respondents. For example, in Adams's (1987) study of elderly female residents of a middle-class Chicago suburb, respondents listed an average of 10 friends according to their own definitions. Three years later they listed an average of 12.2 friends. Older women in a midwestern city reported an average of 5.6 close friends (Babchuk & Anderson, 1989). In a sample of widows, only 60% of whom were 65 years old or older, Lopata (1979) reported an average of 1.25 friends per widow.

A few investigators examined predictors of the size of older adults' friendship networks. Within a nursing home those who had greater lucidity and better vision and speech had more friends. Gender did not affect the number of friends in this context (Retsinas & Garrity, 1985). Among community dwelling older adults participants in social activities had more friends than did nonparticipants (Spakes, 1979), and employed women had more friends than did other older women (Babchuk & Anderson, 1989). Although widows older than 75 years of age had fewer friends than widows aged 65 to 74, the number of married women's friends did not differ by age (Babchuk & Anderson, 1989).

Homogeneity

Very little research has been done on friendship network homogeneity among the elderly. Two exceptions are a study of Jefferson County, Kentucky, (Usui, 1984) and a study of two municipalities in the Netherlands (Dykstra, 1990). Usui reported that both black and white elderly persons had networks characterized by relatively low levels of homogeneity on the dimensions of age, marital status, and education, but high levels of sex and race homogeneity (Usui, 1984). Blacks had networks that were less homogeneous in terms of marital status than their white counterparts, but blacks' and whites' networks did not differ on the other types of homogeneity. All five types of homogeneity were more common among well educated people than among others.

Dykstra (1990) reported on age, generation, gender, and partner status homogeneity. In general, best friends were more homogeneous than friends, who were in turn more homogeneous than close acquaintances, who were more homogeneous than superficial acquaintances.

The research by Usui and Dykstra provides support for Fischer's (1982) observation that people in the minority are more likely to have heterogeneous networks than are people in the majority. Usui reported that the older people were, the less homogeneous their networks were in terms of age, presumably because of the decreasing availability of age peers. Both Usui (1984) and Dykstra (1990) found that men's networks were less homogeneous on the dimension of sex than women's, a result of the gender difference in life expectancy.

Two additional studies confirmed that women's friendship networks are gender homogeneous. Assessing older, midwestern, urban women, Babchuk and Anderson (1989) reported that only about one-fifth of the married or widowed women considered one or more males as friends. In her study of elderly female residents of a middle-class Chicago suburb, Adams (1985) reported a very similar proportion.

Density and Configuration

In an earlier report on Adams's work (Adams, 1983) and in Bear's (1990) study of nursing home residents, the researchers used different questions to establish the existence of a link between network members. Adams (1983) measured two types of density, acquaintanceship density (where a link was recorded if two of the respondent's friends knew one another) and friendship density (where a link was recorded if the respondent perceived two of her friends as friends with one another). Bear (1990) recorded a link for the members of pairs that regularly interacted with one another.

In Adams's (1983) sample the average acquaintanceship density was 42.4%, and the average friendship density was 27.4%. Half of the women lived in age-segregated housing. The density of their networks was not significantly different from that of women residing in the community. The predictors of density in the two types of setting were, however, different. Among the women in age-integrated settings, those with physically limiting conditions had low-density acquaintanceship and friendship networks. Among the women in age-segregated settings, physical condition was not related to either measure of density. This was because women in age-segregated housing listed many friends who lived in the same building. Furthermore, in age-integrated settings both forms of density tended to be positively correlated with the use of various forms of transportation. Women who could travel away from home continued to participate in groups of friends, the members of which were friends with one another or at least knew one another. In contrast, in age-segregated settings, the opposite relationship was found. Women who used various forms of transportation maintained ties with friends who lived elsewhere and thus were not part of the dense building networks on which their less mobile peers were dependent for friendship.

The contact density among friends in the nursing home studied by Bear (1990) was quite high (75.1%). Although her measure of density differed from that of Adams (1983), it was roughly similar to the latter's measure of acquaintanceship density. As one would expect given the differences in the homogeneity and physical conditions of the residents, density was highest in the nursing home environment, next highest in age-segregated housing, and lowest in the age-integrated community setting.

Solidarity

Although many researchers have examined whether older adults have a close friend or one in whom they can confide, only a couple have measured the intimacy characteristic of specific friendships. Usui (1984) asked his respondents to describe each of their three closest friends as very close, somewhat close, or just an acquaintance. Not surprisingly the respondents considered most of their friends as very close. Average closeness was significantly higher in networks that were more homogeneous in terms of age and sex.

In her study of elderly women, Adams (1985-1986) found greater variation in response to a similar question, because she asked them about their feelings of closeness to each of their friends rather than targeting only their three closest friends. Roughly one-third of the friends they named fell into each of the categories. She reported a counter-intuitive finding: The farther away a friend lived from the respondent, the more likely the pair was to be emotionally close. This result occurred because the respondents tended to have known their physically distant friends longer.

❧ Gender and the Life Course

In this section we compare the structural characteristics of friendship across life course stage and gender. For each structural characteristic (size, homogeneity, density, and solidarity), when possible given the existence of relevant research, we address the following questions: Does this characteristic of friendship networks vary over the life course? Is this characteristic related to other network characteristics differently during different stages of the life course? Are the predictors of this characteristic different at different stages of the life course? And, finally, do women and men differ in this aspect of friendship structure, and, if so, does gender affect this characteristic differently across stages of the life course?

Size

The number of friends does not vary much across the life course. The studies of specific life course stages, cited previously, showed that the average number of friends reported for college students is between 2.88 and 9.1 (Johnson & Leslie, 1982; Wister & Avison, 1982); for adults it is 6.0 (Weiss & Lowenthal, 1975); and for older adults it is between 1 and 12.2 (Adams, 1987; Retsinas & Garrity, 1985). The greater range reported for older adults is an artifact of the samples studied—residents of nursing homes and age-segregated housing have age peers readily available for friendship. In a study of people in grades 2 through 8 and from 15 to 65 years of age, Reisman and Shorr (1978) reported no differences in the number of friends claimed after grade 3. Similarly, Nahemow and Lawton (1975) found no differences in the size of the network of old (1.9 friends), middle-aged (2.5 friends), and young (2.4 friends) city housing project residents. In contrast to the findings of other studies, Weiss and Lowenthal (1975) reported that the number of friends fluctuated across the life course (newlyweds were more likely to list both members of a couple as friends, whereas the older respondents listed only the same-sex member), but they did not test for significance of the differences.

One cannot compare various predictors of network size across the life course, because studies of the friendships of people at different stages of the life course have included different variables. For example, researchers have examined how romantic involvement influenced size of young adult networks (Fischer et al., 1989; Johnson &

Leslie, 1982; Milardo, 1982) and how lucidity, vision, and speech affected size of older adult networks (Retsinas & Garrity, 1985).

The findings on the effect of gender on friendship network size across the life course are mixed. College women appear to have more friends than college men (Johnson & Leslie, 1982; Peretti, 1976), but the results for gender differences among other adults are mixed. In their study of blue-collar respondents Weiss and Lowenthal (1975) reported that, at all stages, women consistently claimed a greater number of friends than did men. In contrast, Booth and Hess (1974) found that white-collar men had more friends than white-collar women had, but blue-collar men and women did not differ on number of friends.

This discrepancy might be the result of the difference in the age composition of the samples. In an examination of the Northern California data Fischer and Oliker (1983) found that young single men and women named the same number of nonkin associates; adult men named more than adult women named; and elderly women identified more friends than did elderly men. The authors explained the gender differences mainly in structural terms. During the adult years men have more incentives and opportunities for work-related friendships, and women have less time because of motherhood. Structural changes in the life course, however, reduce the friendship opportunities for men and the constraints on women. Due to differential mortality of men and women and the tendency of people to choose friends of their same sex, older women have more friendship candidates available than older men have.

Homogeneity

Researchers have focused on homogeneity in adult friendship networks much more than in friendship networks at other stages of life, so information on which to base life course comparisons is scant. Nahemow and Lawton (1975) did report, however, that old and young people were more likely than middle-aged people to select friends similar to themselves in terms of age and race. In addition, Weiss and Lowenthal (1975) reported that four fifths of their respondents, at every stage of life, had a similar-aged closest friend.

The majority of people's friends were of the same sex, but opposite-sex friends were reported most frequently by the young.

Three predictors of network homogeneity—the degree of homogeneity of the context, status, and gender—have been examined for different life course stages. There is mixed and scant evidence for college students (Bochner, Hutnik, & Furnham, 1985; Furnham & Alibhai, 1985; Ting-Toomey, 1981), strong evidence for adults (Feld, 1982; Fischer, 1982; McPherson & Smith-Lovin, 1987), and apparently no evidence for the elderly that the degree of homogeneity of the context affects friendship network homogeneity. During both adulthood and old age high-status people tend to have more homogeneous networks than low-status people (Jackson, 1977; Laumann, 1973; Schutte & Light, 1978; Usui, 1984; Verbrugge, 1977). Men have less gender-homogeneous networks than women have, both during adulthood (Booth & Hess, 1974) and old age (Dykstra, 1990; Usui, 1984).

Density

Friendship network density apparently does not vary much across the life course. Researchers have reported friendship network density as 37.9% for college students (Wister & Avison, 1982), lower than 44% for adults (Fischer, 1982), and between 27.4% and 42.4% for older adults (Adams, 1983). The only estimate that was significantly different was for nursing home residents, who had very dense networks (75.1%; Bear, 1990).

One cannot compare predictors of friendship density across the life course because different predictors were examined for different stages of life. For example, the focus with adults was the effects of status on friendship network density (Laumann, 1973), whereas the emphasis with older adults was the effects of physical condition and transportation use patterns on friendship network density (Adams, 1983). Gender differences in friendship network density have apparently not been studied at any stage of the life course.

Solidarity

The majority of the studies of friendship network solidarity have been of college students, so comparisons across life course stages are difficult to make. One research team, however, reported no differences in network solidarity among female high school students, teachers, and retired teachers (Candy, Troll, & Levy, 1981).

Scholars who have studied network solidarity among college students found that women's networks were higher in solidarity than were those of men (Barth & Kinder, 1988; Johnson & Leslie, 1982). Hess (1979) predicted the same relationship for mature adults and the elderly.

ᴥ Summary and Research Implications

Despite the recent trend toward studying friendship as a relationship rather than as a collection of attributes of individuals and the concomitant focus on network structure (see Chapter 2), full-fledged studies of friendship structure are still relatively rare. Few personal network analysts have concerned themselves with whether a particular tie is with a friend or another type of associate. Many other researchers used the term *network* when they employed global measures of variables such as solidarity rather than considering the form of specific ties.

Comparisons across studies are difficult, if not impossible, to make. Researchers have focused on different topics depending on which age group they sampled. Even when investigators studied the same aspects of friendship structure, they did not use the same measures. Some researchers sampled special populations rather than general ones. All of these factors make it difficult to synthesize the information on friendship structure and to build on it.

The effects of age and gender on friendship structure have not been adequately studied. Many investigators included members of only one gender or one age group. Others collected the data that would have made comparisons possible but did not perform them. Still others examined gender and age differences but did not develop theoretical explanations for the findings. None of the studies reviewed in this chapter were designed to demonstrate whether the effects of age and gender were attributable to differences in social structural position or in psychological disposition.

Certain aspects of friendship structure have not been studied at all (e.g., status and power hierarchy in friendship). With a few exceptions (e.g., Johnsen, 1986; Salzinger, 1982), the scholars of adult friendship structure have focused either on the dyad or on the network but not on the links between the two levels of analysis. Finally, the literature on the connections among friendship structure and the other elements of friendship patterns (processes and phases) is so sparse that we did not review it here. In the next two chapters, however, we review the literature on processes and phases themselves.

4

Friendship Processes

The second component of friendship patterns is friendship processes, which encompass cognitive, affective, and behavioral categories as well as proxy measures. This chapter includes a review of research on various friendship processes at three stages of the adult life cycle, followed by a comparison of processes across genders and the life course. Although interaction processes have been studied widely in laboratory experiments among people meeting for the first time and in ongoing romantic relationships, relatively little research on the operation of processes in friendship exists. Moreover, the various processes have not been studied comprehensively across age groups or with the same measures, so for the most part it is not possible to compare specific processes of college student, adult, and old-age friendships. Also few studies of network processes have been conducted, so it is difficult to compare dyadic and network processes.

The processes that adults use in their friendship interactions are influenced by social structure and the historical context (see Chapter 1), the structural features of the dyads and networks in which they participate (see Chapter 3), their previous experiences in close relationships, their developmental maturity, and their personality characteristics. We urge readers to keep these interacting sets of influences in mind as they ponder the implications of the studies reviewed in this chapter, even though researchers seldom interpret their findings in light of these influences.

We remind readers again of the caveats about the literature on adult friendship mentioned at the beginning of Chapter 3. Also relevant to this chapter are the discussions in Chapter 3 about the characteristics that distinguish young, middle-aged, and older adults from each other. Just as all these issues affect the literature on friendship structure, so do they influence the findings on processes.

❧ College Student Friendships

Studies of young adult friendship processes are based on college student samples (as we found in Chapter 3 for studies of dyadic and network structure). In the following pages we review studies of various cognitive, affective, and behavioral processes, and proxy indicators of them, among college-student friends.

Cognitive Processes

Conceptions of friendship. How do people define friendship and know that it exists (see Chapter 1)? Research on characteristics that define the essential nature of friendship relations provides an answer to this question. For example, according to a phenomenological study of women, friendship included: a loving relationship; a world of shared meanings and understandings; ongoing growth and change; the interrelated attributes of concern, sharing, commitment, freedom, respect, trust, and equality; and promotion of personal development (Becker, 1987). Men also defined friendship in terms of trust and intimacy, but emphasized instrumental activity more than women did (Swain, 1989).

Another perspective on conceptions of friendship comes from the attempts of Murstein and Spitz (1973-74) and Bukowski et al. (1987) to validate Aristotle's typology of friendship among contemporary college students. The results showed that young adults differentiated among Aristotle's three dimensions of friendship across types of friends, although their actual friendships failed to match the Aristotelian ideal. Males differentiated between their same- and opposite-sex friends to a greater extent than did females. Males emphasized affective aspects of friendship (goodness and enjoyableness) with their female friends more than with their male friends. Taken together, the results of these two studies show that, in general, students' perceptions of friendship were in accord with Aristotle's philosophical discourse.

Several researchers used vignettes of resource exchanges to investigate perception of the existence of friendship, attribution of the degree of solidarity between friends, and prediction of future closeness of friends (Clark, 1981; Törnblom & Fredholm, 1984; Törnblom, Fredholm, & Jonsson, 1987). In general, respondents made differential attributions of current and future closeness depending on the types of resources exchanged and the current closeness of the relationship. These findings show that young adults could interpret observed signs of friendship even when they had only minimal information about the relationship.

Information processing. The strategies that individuals use to learn and remember information can affect friendship patterns. Meeting new people and developing friendships require assimilation, retention, and recall of many kinds of information. Of relevance here is the observation that information processing differs across genders. Banikiotes, Neimeyer, and Lepkowsky (1981) reviewed previous research showing that sex-role orientation influenced information processing about relationships and that males used different cognitive strategies to select their male and female friends whereas females did not. In their own study, however, Banikiotes et al. found that gender was more influential than sex-role orientation in its impact on the descriptions of ideal female versus ideal male friends, with males exhibiting greater description differences than females.

One aspect of information processing is memory, which also affects friendship patterns. Duck, Pond, and Leatham (1991) found that recall of events in relationships is influenced by partners' cognitions, feelings, and perceptions of the relationship and by interactions with each other. Friends recalled their interaction as having been less positive than they had rated it initially, and their recollections were significantly influenced by their present feelings about their relationship.

Person perception. When individuals first meet they form impressions of each other based on social group and physical characteristics, and they tend to attribute stereotyped traits to each other. As people get to know each other better, they discover and respond to each other's unique personality characteristics; stereotypes become less influential in the relationship. Research on person perception has focused both on the accuracy with which people perceive others and on the accuracy of people's predictions of how others see them.

Several researchers examined person perception in the context of friendship. Henderson and Furnham (1982a) showed that persons thought to be popular by others described themselves differently on traits such as locus of control and neuroticism than those deemed unpopular. The descriptions of close friends versus acquaintances also differed on perceived traits. Kernis and Wheeler (1981) found that individuals were rated positively when they were in the presence of an unattractive nonfriend or an attractive friend, but not when they were with an unattractive friend. Apparently the raters assumed that a person with an attractive friend must possess favorable qualities but someone with an unattractive friend must not.

Malloy and Albright (1990) examined the issue that perceptions of another are influenced not only by the characteristics of the other, but also by the characteristics of the perceiver. They found support for this contention among well-acquainted dorm roommates. They also found, as did Henderson and Furnham (1982b), that the students did not perceive themselves as similar to each other. They pointed out that the assumption of similarity among friends is based on research conducted with unacquainted individuals. Strangers are likely to select as potential friends persons who are similar in superficial ways that are less important to well-acquainted pairs.

Attraction and similarity. Friendship is based on attraction of partners for one another, and attraction is based in part on perceived similarity of personality, values, attitudes, beliefs, needs, or social skills between partners. Many studies of attraction and similarity are not relevant for our purposes, however, because their research designs called for brief interactions between new acquaintances under contrived experimental conditions or requested respondents' reactions to hypothetical persons. Also some researchers operationalized attraction indirectly by assessing degree of solidarity, rather than directly by asking questions about what contributes to attraction. Relatively few studies of attraction and similarity in naturally occurring established friendships have been conducted.

When asked about important characteristics of friends, respondents spontaneously offer similarity as a salient dimension (e.g., Weiss & Lowenthal, 1975). Werner and Parmelee (1979) reported that although friends were more interested in similar activities than were strangers, attitudes were as dissimilar between friends as they were between strangers. Henderson and Furnham (1982b) found that personality similarity was not a strong basis for choice of friends, but that friends did have similar needs and beliefs. Although the friends in the Werner and Parmelee (1979) study perceived that they were more similar on attitudes than they actually were, those friends examined by Henderson and Furnham (1982b) did not. Werner and Parmelee (1979) suggested that shared activity preferences may set the stage for the further development of friendship, which will occur only if the partners discover that they share similar attitudes and values as well as interests. In testing the hypothesis that similarity is differentially important across phases of friendship, McCarthy and Duck (1976) found that in recently formed friendships students were more attracted to friends who purportedly (via experimental manipulation) had somewhat dissimilar attitudes than to those who were apparently totally similar to themselves. In established friendships, though, they preferred friends with similar attitudes.

Does similarity, in fact, undergird liking over time? It seems to do so for females but not males. Hill and Stull (1981) investigated this connection during an academic year. The degree of value similarity in the fall among female college students who had *chosen* each other as roommates was high. It was correlated with their liking for each other in the fall and with their predicted liking scores in the spring. Value similarity in the fall among females who were *assigned* to be roommates was lower and was predictive only of their still being roommates in the spring, not their liking. These relationships were not statistically significant for the males.

Self-monitoring. Persons who are high in self-monitoring attempt to control the image of themselves that they present to others so that it is appropriate for each type of situation, even if their behavior does not reflect their attitudes. Those who are low in self-monitoring typically display their actual dispositions and attitudes in various situations, such that their behavior tends to match their attitudes. Snyder, Gangestad, and Simpson (1983) reported confirmation of these premises in research on reasons for choosing friends for particular activities. High self-monitoring individuals interacted with specific friends in specific contexts, selecting the activity partners on the basis of their skills or other characteristics relevant to the activity at hand. Low self-monitoring persons, instead, selected friends on the basis of their general characteristics and likability, regardless of the activity they were going to pursue. Snyder et al. (1983) pointed out that these differing tendencies probably result from distinct conceptions of friendship (activity-based versus affect-based).

Differences in self-monitoring have implications for the size of one's friend network, the extent of attachment to friends, the range of activities shared with each friend, the effects of loss of a given friendship, and the feelings of the person selected to be a friend about participating in the relationship. Rather than assuming that all people are friends with those whom they like the best (see the next subsection on affective processes), it may be that such a generalization is true only for low self-monitoring persons (Snyder et al., 1983).

Relationship monitoring. Besides monitoring the self in social interactions, people also keep track of what goes on in their relationships.

Clark and Mills (1979) proposed that in exchange relationships (with strangers, acquaintances, business contacts), individuals have no special obligation toward each other beyond giving and receiving comparable benefits as defined by the type of relationship. In contrast, communal relationships (with family, friends, romantic partners) involve the partners in special, ongoing responsibilities toward each other, but they are not obliged to return benefits comparable to those they just received. The implication, confirmed by lab experiments, is that people monitor their friendships less strictly than they monitor less close relationships. College students were more inclined to keep track of their own inputs in a problem-solving task under exchange than under communal relationship conditions (Clark, 1984) and they displayed greater concern for friends' needs than for strangers' needs (Clark, Mills, & Corcoran, 1989).

Affective Processes

Liking. Liking and disliking are two separate constructs, according to Rodin (1978), and the criteria for liking or disliking someone are different from whether or not certain characteristics or behaviors are favored. Rodin argued that the reason friends do not begin to dislike each other even after they have revealed negative information about themselves is that people who possess disliked qualities are not selected as friends in the first place. Friends who are liked may indeed have negative qualities, but those negative qualities are not relevant to the criteria for selecting friends. Thus discovery of such negative qualities over the course of the friendship does not necessarily diminish liking for the friend.

Hill and Stull (1981) reported that correlates of liking among college roommates in the fall were closeness, perceived likelihood of staying in touch after graduation, interaction time, self-disclosure, having chosen each other as roommates, and perceived similarity (but not actual value similarity). Predictors of liking among roommates in the spring were ratings of relationship quality, interaction indices, and perceived similarity in the fall. As indicated earlier, actual similarity in the fall predicted liking in the spring for women but not for men.

Satisfaction. Studies show that intimacy and positive interactions with friends are important to satisfaction with friends for both sexes, but some differences in correlates of satisfaction occur. For example, Jones (1991) reported that female students had greater trust in male friends, a more communal orientation to assistance, and higher satisfaction than did male students. There were no sex differences in trust of female friends. For both females and males trust in male friends enhanced satisfaction but an exchange orientation diminished it. Also for both sexes significant predictors of satisfaction were self-disclosure and enjoyment.

In one of the few studies of network processes, Hirsch (1980) examined satisfaction with friendship networks. The significant predictors were the students' satisfaction with their multiplex friendships, not having fixed roles in the friendships, having a group feeling when together with friend network members, and engaging in a variety of activities with them. Hirsch concluded that relationships that promote diversity also promote personal growth, which makes them satisfying.

Behavioral Processes

Expressions of affection. In Chapter 3 we indicated that solidarity, or degree of closeness, is a structural feature of friendship. Here we discuss research on how friends reveal and express this closeness toward each other.

The main focus of research on expressions of affection is gender differences. For example, Williams (1985) found that male students were less likely than female students to confide in their close friends, express feelings related to vulnerability, display affection toward male friends, emphasize understanding and responsibility aspects of friendship, or discuss personal issues. Also males were more likely than females to share activities than to converse with their friends. Aukett, Ritchie, and Mill (1988) replicated these results with respect to same-sex friends in a sample of college students in New Zealand. In addition, they found that men, but not women, relied on their opposite-sex friends for emotional support.

Both males and females who were higher on femininity in the Williams (1985) study had emotionally closer friendships than those who were lower on femininity; masculinity was not related to friendship intimacy. Nevertheless, Williams concluded that even males with a high degree of femininity were inhibited from behaving in expressive ways with their male friends.

Swain (1989) also found that internalized constraints on expression of emotion led men to favor a more active style of conveying intimacy than the verbal forms used by women. When the male students interacted with their close friends, they did participate in self-disclosure. But more commonly they exchanged favors, engaged in competitive activities, joked, touched, included each other in activities, talked about their accomplishments, shared resources, and taught skills as signs of their favorable regard for each other.

The gender differences described in the above three studies also endured over the four years of an investigation conducted by Griffin and Sparks (1990). Female-female friend pairs remained closer over time than male-male pairs. The male-female dyads had the lowest scores on the closeness index, illustrating the strong norms against cross-sex friendship in American society.

Communication. Self-disclosure, an important aspect of friendship, has been studied in terms of the extent to which the level of intimacy in one person's message is reciprocated by another, how self-disclosure varies with solidarity, and how it differs for females and males.

As with similarity and liking, reciprocation of self-disclosure intimacy operates differently in new and ongoing friendships. Derlega, Wilson, and Chaikin (1976) found that students were more likely to reciprocate a high level of intimacy when it was initiated by a stranger than when it was initiated by a friend, probably because friends assume they will have other opportunities for intimate communication.

Rather than comparing disclosure with friends versus strangers, Won-Doornink (1985) investigated reciprocity of self-disclosure for cross-sex friends at three levels of closeness and compared American and Korean students. In general, nonintimate disclosures showed a linear decrease from acquaintance to best friend. Intimate disclosures followed a curvilinear pattern reflecting low levels with acquaintances and best friends and a higher number with friends. This pattern of findings occurred in both nationalities, showing the strength of self-disclosure reciprocity despite the fact that teenagers and college students in South Korea do not socialize with the opposite sex or date to the extent that they do in the United States.

Along with variation in conversational intimacy, other aspects of conversation are different across types of relationships. Duck, Rutt, Hurst, and Strejc (1991) reported that best friends, friends, acquaintances, lovers, relatives, and strangers can be distinguished from one another on the basis of everyday communication patterns and outcomes. For example, conversations with best friends were rated highest on communication quality and third highest on value and were deemed unlikely to change the relationship. Conversations with friends were rated a little lower on quality and value but still were unlikely to affect the future of the friendship, especially for males. The authors suggested that results from laboratory studies, implying that conversations lead to relationship changes, may not apply to ongoing friendships.

Another area of inquiry in communication patterns is sex differences in self-disclosure. According to Reisman (1990), both males and females, in the United States and Hungary, believe that females reveal more about their feelings and problems than do males. Similarly, Johnson and Aries (1983a) found that females conversed more frequently and in greater depth than males about themselves and their close relationships; the focus of male conversations was activity-oriented topics. For both females and males, however, conversations with close, same-sex friends concerned the self, relationships, and daily activities. The authors interpreted this pattern in terms of the contributions of such conversations to the young adults' identity formation process. Indeed Snell (1989) found a relationship between level of social anxiety and topic of conversation. Persons who were high on social anxiety were less willing to discuss personal information that was inconsistent with their gender role with same-sex than with opposite-sex friends. They were more willing to discuss gender role-consistent information with their same-sex friends.

Conflict. Some conflict strategies promote growth of relationships, but others interfere with relationship harmony. Canary and Cupach (1988) found that integrative conflict tactics (seeking areas of agreement, negotiating, and expressing trust) yielded communication satisfaction which in turn was associated with trust, intimacy, and relationship satisfaction. On the other hand, distributive strategies (competition, hostility, demands, and threats) resulted in decreased trust. Finally, avoidance strategies (denying or being ambiguous about the conflict or changing the subject) could be either constructive or destructive. Although perceived use of such tactics by one's partner did not have an impact on the evaluation of the relationship, Canary and Cupach (1988) found that avoidance strategies diminished the relational satisfaction of the partner who used them.

Healey and Bell (1990) adopted Rusbult's (1987) conceptual framework in their study of students' responses to dissatisfaction with friends and the involvement of their friend network in disputes with friends. Healey and Bell found no differences between females and males on the extent to which they employed each of four conflict management strategies [exit (ending or threatening to end the friendship), voice (discussing problems or changing behavior to resolve them), loyalty (passively waiting for the relationship to improve), or neglect (passively allowing the friendship to wither)]. Females, compared to males, were more likely to discuss their conflicts with other friends, received advice about dealing with conflict from a greater proportion of their networks, and rated their conflicts as more serious and as having a more harmful impact on the friendship. Males believed that their network members would oppose ending the problematic friendship more strongly than females did. Nevertheless, the network had relatively little impact on dyadic responses to friendship dissatisfaction. These and other outcomes in Healey and Bell's report underscore the value of Rusbult's theory for future research on friendship conflict.

Social support. If people expect to receive support from their friends, they must be willing and able to seek it. Shapiro (1980) found that help seeking was more frequent between friends than between strangers. Moreover, students were less likely to seek help from a stranger if the cost of giving it was high than if the cost was low; this difference did not occur in seeking help from a friend. It may be that temporary imbalances in friendship exchanges are not important because friends expect to have opportunities to reciprocate each other's help in the future.

Focusing on the exchange process associated with social support, Hays (1989) examined benefits and costs experienced in interactions with close and casual friends. Regarding benefits, students reported that close friends provided more emotional support and information than casual friends supplied; the two categories of friends did not differ on fun and relaxation, help with tasks, or intellectual stimulation. Receipt of such benefits was highly correlated with feeling closer to or more positive toward friends. On the other hand, costs (wasted time, boredom, irritation) diminished feelings of closeness to casual but not close friends. As indicated in the section on liking above, it may be that people are willing to accept some negative qualities in closer friends because the benefits such friends give are more important than these costs.

Gender differences occur in social support. For example, Buhrke and Fuqua (1987) found that in same-sex relationships, female in contrast to male students had more contact when under stress; were closer; were more satisfied with how the relationships were initiated, with the balance of give and take and with the level of closeness; and perceived that they knew their friends better and were better known by friends. In cross-sex relationships females initiated more and wanted to give more than did males. On the other hand, males were closer to their cross-sex supporters than were females. Finally, both groups wanted to have more frequent contact and closeness and wanted to give more in cross-sex than in same-sex relationships.

Proxy Measures of Process

Quantity of interaction. Most research reports on friendship mention the length of acquaintance and frequency of contact only in passing, if at all. Investigations of students' friendships typically concern new friends made at college, not long-standing friendships.

Thus in the studies cited above that assessed length of acquaintance, the participants had known their friends for an average of 6 to 14 months (Henderson & Furnham, 1982a, 1982b; Malloy & Albright, 1990; McCarthy & Duck, 1976). Several researchers, however, investigated longer-standing friendships. The male-male pairs in the Griffin and Sparks (1990) study had been friends for an average of 30 months, and the respondents in Werner and Parmelee's (1979) study had known each other for an average of 5 years.

Hays (1989) compared close and casual friends on a number of interaction characteristics. Close friends reported more interactions; more days, times, and locations of interactions; a smaller proportion of brief interactions; greater proportions of deliberately arranged interactions and home versus campus settings of interactions; and more exclusive interactions than casual friends reported.

Variety of processes. Most of the friendship process research focuses on just one process. Thus researchers generally have not inquired about multiplexity, the range of shared activities, or directionality, the type of reciprocity in friendship. Evidence of multiplexity in the Hays (1989) study was the finding that the amounts of fun and relaxation, emotional support, and information or advice were all correlated with positive effects of interactions, implying that a diversity of enjoyable activities is important in friendship. Women viewed their supportive relationships as more complex than men viewed theirs (Buhrke & Fuqua, 1987), and women preferred friends to whom they could relate in many different ways whereas men developed different relationships to meet different needs (Barth & Kinder, 1988).

With regard to directionality, Hays (1989) examined both emotional support and information or advice given and received. Although he did not report tests of significance, inspection of the means shows that they were nearly identical across close and casual friendships and male and female respondents, except that females reported giving more emotional support than they received. These results suggest that the friendships of college students tend to be reciprocal. In Buhrke and Fuqua's (1987) study, women had a relatively equal balance of give and take in both their same- and cross-sex relationships and were satisfied with the balance. Men reported giving more in their same-sex than in their cross-sex relationships and were less satisfied than women with the balance of give and take.

Wright (1982) reported patterns of interaction for females and males similar to those described above. He pointed out, however, that these findings must be considered along with length of the friendship and depth of closeness. He found that sex differences diminished in close, long-term friendships.

ِ Adult Friendships

The literature on adult friendship processes is not extensive, and processes used by middle-aged adults have been neglected. As was the case in Chapter 3, the studies described below include a wide range of respondent ages, from as young as 18 to as old as the early 60s. We identified a few reports on each of the three process categories and on proxy indicators of process.

Cognitive Processes

Attraction and similarity. Similarity of values and interests were important predictors of friendship in adulthood, along with politeness, friendliness, and being easy to talk to (Johnson, 1989). Shared political ideology was deemed important by female feminists (Rose & Roades, 1987). Also adult friends may select each other at least partly on the basis of genetic similarity. Rushton (1989) found that males were more similar to their friends than to randomly paired others in conservative attitudes, feelings of altruism and intimacy, and personality.

Relationship analyzing. In contrast to the discussion of an individual's relationship monitoring in the section on college student friendship, here we focus on how friends help each other interpret relationships. Oliker's (1989) account of best friend relations among married women represents an example of network-level process. Friends helped each other analyze their marriages; talking with each other about problems with their husbands led them to think about situations in new ways. Such reformulation of the issues often enabled the women to eliminate negative thinking and emotional reactions and find effective ways to handle their concerns. Although this example illustrates the effects of thinking about one's spousal relationship, the same process applies to friendship when, for instance, one person helps another to think through problems with a friend.

Affective Processes

Satisfaction. Contributors to friendship satisfaction among adults were instrumental reward (e.g., working on a joint task, respecting privacy, giving advice), emotional support, and shared interests. The factors describing emotional support and shared interests were especially important. Opposite-sex friends had lower satisfaction ratings than same-sex friends, but showed a similar pattern of ratings (Argyle & Furnham, 1983).

Trust. Contrary to expectations based on the fact that women disclose more to their friends than do men, the men in Davidson and Duberman's (1982) study had higher levels of trust for their best friends than the women had. But the men talked about impersonal, less risky topics more than the women did. Thus the results for trust must be interpreted in light of the fact that although the men perceived they were being open and trusting, this occurred on a superficial level because they actually invested little in the personal and interactional aspects of the friendship.

Emotion management. Besides helping each other analyze their friendships, friends can also help each other manage their feelings. Oliker (1989) provided examples of such network-level affective processes. Women reported that they were able to talk about their feelings with friends, who by allowing the expression of volatile emotions, helped them diffuse their reactions in a safe and effective manner. For example, a woman could express anger about someone in another relationship to a friend without escalating the conflict or damaging the other relationship. Best friends helped women manage their emotional reactions while acknowledging and affirming the reality of the feelings, thus reducing stress.

Behavioral Processes

Activities. Friends enjoy spending time together—what do they do? Morse and Marks (1985) queried adults on Australian beaches to investigate types of interactions in two categories of friendship, *mates* and *friends.* Although respondents engaged in social activities as frequently with mates as with friends, relations with mates were more activity-specific. Reciprocal discussion of personal problems and reciprocal visiting in each other's homes was more common with friends, whereas borrowing and lending money was more central to relations with mates. Over all activities, the mean for females was higher than that for males. Also males reported engaging in activities more frequently with mates than with friends, but for females there were no differences in frequency of interaction.

Communication. Talk cements friendships in adulthood, as least for women. When Johnson and Aries (1983b) asked women about the most important benefit of their friendships, respondents highlighted the value of conversation, either by itself or along with other shared activities. Female friends were valued for listening noncritically, providing support that enhanced feelings of self-esteem, validating experiences, offering comfort, and contributing to personal growth.

Several researchers compared women's and men's communication patterns in friendship. In terms of the content of conversations, women discussed topical, relational, and personal material with friends, but men focused on the topical level (Davidson & Duberman, 1982). Women were more likely than men to speak with their friends on the phone for 10 minutes or more, talk in depth about personal problems, reveal doubts and fears, and discuss intimate relationships (Aries & Johnson, 1983). The results suggest that sex-role patterns influence the conversational topics and depth in adult friendship.

Tschann (1988) discovered that sex roles were not the only determinants of gender differences in disclosure to friends. Marital status seemed to play a part for men because married men disclosed less on intimate topics to their friends than did unmarried men or either married or unmarried women. With low-intimacy topics, married people disclosed less than unmarried people did, regardless of their sex.

Conflict. Several of the scholars cited above also examined relational conflict. For example, Argyle and Furnham (1983) identified sources of conflict, labeling the first factor *emotional* (e.g., competition, conflict over beliefs and values, conflict over the social group) and the second *criticism* (e.g., conflict over habits, life-style, or personal problems). Within same-sex friendships conflict was fairly low for criticism items and higher for emotional items related to competition and differing beliefs and values. Conflict was slightly lower with opposite-sex friends than with same-sex friends. Davidson and Duberman (1982) found that conflict was low in best friend dyads for both men and women. Overall, however, men reported more conflict in their relationships than did women. The authors interpreted this finding as confirming the assumption that women have been socialized to suppress or avoid conflict.

Social support. Many expressions of support are possible between friends. In an unusual example, O'Connell (1984) studied the ways that owner-builders of their own homes handled the help with house construction that they received from friends. The majority of the exchanges were unbalanced, but that did not diminish the friendships because norms other than strict reciprocity were operative in these relationships. Many respondents believed either that payment for the help was unnecessary or that balance would be achieved some time in the future. The Need Norm (planning to reciprocate if the friend needs help in the future) and the Norm of Noninstrumental Concern (assuming that the friend helped out of altruism and not desire for personal gain) were operative and were beneficial to the friendships.

Proxy Measures of Process

Quantity of interaction. Respondents in the Morse and Marks (1985) study had known their mates and friends for similar periods (8.6 and 9.3 years on average), had been mates or friends for nearly equivalent periods (means of 7.95 and 8.2 years), and spent about 7.5 hours a week with each type of friend. The women in Rose and Roades's (1987) study had known their friends 5 or 6 years on average.

In her study of women's best friends, Oliker (1989) reported frequent visiting (at least a few times a week for the majority) and telephoning (from a few times a week to nearly every day) between these friends. Similarly, Rose and Roades's (1987) respondents saw their friends between 1.28 and 2.19 times a week on average. Aries and Johnson (1983) noted that 50% of the women but only 19% of the men in their study had daily or weekly phone conversations with their close friend.

Verbrugge (1983) provided data on predictors of contact with best friends, from males in the United States and both sexes in Germany. Age, marital status, and occupation were the strongest predictors of friend contact. Young and elderly adults, never-married people, students, production workers, and sales workers were the categories of respondents with the most contact. Friends with the same marital status and political preference saw each other more than those who were dissimilar in these respects, but those who differed on age, sex, religious preference, and residential stability saw each other more than those who were the same on these variables. The strongest predictor of contact was being neighbors; greater residential proximity and affection contributed to higher frequency of contact. Finally, length of acquaintance was inversely related to frequency of contact.

Variety of processes. Jackson et al. (1977) constructed an index of multiplexity by counting the number of role relations (friend, kin, coworker, and so on) between each respondent and each of his friends. Links with just one role relation—friends—amounted to 26% of the total. Some 43% of the links involved two roles, 26% involved three roles, 6% were associated in four ways, and almost none interacted in five ways. The researchers concluded that increased multiplexity did not affect the quality of friendship because multiplexity was lower for men who knew each other longer, and multiplexity was inversely related to intimacy. Although men who had more multiplex friendships saw each other more often than they saw others, this was only because these friends were also neighbors, and neighbors saw each other more often than did other friend pairs.

We found no data on directionality in adult friendships. The prevalence of reciprocal versus nonreciprocal interaction is unknown, and the individual and dyadic predictors of each type of interaction have not been identified.

❧ Old Age Friendships

The literature contains many studies on the functions of friends in late adulthood and correlates of various forms of friend support. In contrast, there are relatively few studies that addressed friendship processes directly, particularly in the cognitive and affective domains.

Cognitive Processes

Conceptions of friendship. Albert and Moss (1990) had older adults rank attributes of personal relationships according to how well they characterized interaction with friends and relatives. Women's and men's perceptions did not differ significantly, suggesting that they have a common culture of relationships made up of slightly different dimensions. The authors also examined the extent to which respondents agreed with others' perceptions, explaining that shared consensus reflects social integration, which is associated with mental health. They found that sharing in consensus about best friends was significantly associated with women's mental health but not men's.

Another way that older adults conceptualize friendship was discovered by Matthews (1983). Some respondents focused on individuals who possessed certain characteristics and who were considered to be friends, whereas others focused on friendship as a relationship for which many different people might qualify. As discussed in

Chapter 6, these definitions have differing implications for the availability of friends in old age and thus for friendship interventions.

Many early friendship scholars failed to distinguish among levels of solidarity when studying conceptions of friendship. Moreover, comparisons across studies are difficult because of method variance (see Chapters 1 and 3). To address these issues Blieszner (1982, in press) asked each respondent to provide information on very close friends, casual friends, and acquaintances in their network. Based on this within-subjects design, observed differences can be attributed to variation in solidarity, unconfounded with respondent characteristics and measures. The results showed that closest friends were rated significantly higher than the other types on subjective indicators of relationship quality (satisfaction, emotional closeness, and the like) as well as on behavioral dimensions of friendship (such as joint activities and resource exchanges). Clearly, closest friends have a special place in the lives of older adults, and researchers should evaluate level of solidarity along with other variables.

In yet another approach to conceptions of friendship, Adams (1985) explored older women's views of cross-sex friendships. Only about 4% of the friendships described by the respondents were with men, and only 17% of the women had any male friends. When asked why they did not have any or more male friends, the women expressed the belief that cross-sex friendships were preludes to romance, and they cited strong norms against courtship among older adults.

Conceptions of friendship are also revealed by studies of population subgroups. For example, Cohen and Rajkowski (1982) found that among elderly residents of single room occupancy hotels a significant minority had multiplex relationships with nonfriend contacts whom they deemed important and intimate. At the same time respondents rated some of their friends as not important, and respondents did not share intimate thoughts with certain friends. These findings suggest that standard definitions of and assumptions about friendship are not necessarily applicable to all segments of the population. They reinforce our discussion in Chapter 1 about the importance of carefully defining friendship and grounding research questions and variables in theory.

Affective Processes

Enjoyment. Dykstra (1990) found that 79% of her Dutch sample members agreed that they laughed with their friends, and 72% agreed that they had lots of fun with friends.

Satisfaction. Satisfaction with friendship among older adults has received much research attention. Adams (1983) found that women were delighted or pleased with approximately equal proportions of their friendships (31% to 39%) and less than pleased with a smaller proportion (23% to 30%). Respondents were satisfied with their friendships if they had large networks and if at least one friend helped with at least one task, regardless of network size. Also the number of tasks with which friends helped was positively related to the respondents' satisfaction when controlling for the size of their networks.

Indicators of satisfaction with best friendships were general satisfaction, closeness, and satisfaction with self-disclosure and emotional support (Jones & Vaughan, 1990). Conflict and endorsement of a communal orientation were significant predictors of satisfaction, with the former diminishing it and the latter enhancing it. On the other hand, enjoyment, perceived equity, and reciprocity did not predict friendship satisfaction.

Rook (1987) examined the connection between reciprocity of exchanges and relationship satisfaction. Reciprocity was greater in respondents' interactions with friends than with adult children, and it was significantly related to satisfaction with friend but not family relationships. Although Clark and Mills (1979) theorized that communal relationships such as friendship do not involve concern about reciprocity, Rook (1987) pointed out that the Clark and Mills research was conducted in an experimental setting in which subjects became indebted to strangers. In contrast, Rook's (1987) work tapped the degree of mutuality in multiple types of exchanges in ongoing relationships. Therefore in a real-world setting high reciprocity reflected strong, intense relationships characterized by positive feelings rather than indicating the exchange relationships described by Clark and Mills (1979).

Behavioral Processes

Expressions of affection. Affection is displayed differently in new and long-standing friendships. Shea et al. (1988) found that although ongoing exchanges of affection were important in new friendships, relationships with old friends were less dependent on overt exchanges of affection. Even though respondents did not live near their old friends or see them often, they retained strong feelings of affection for them.

Companionship. Friends in old age serve as companions for each other in a variety of ways. Dykstra (1990) found that 76% of respondents often had coffee or tea in network members' homes, and 55% often had dinner with friends. In comparing the confidant and companionship networks of older adults, Connidis and Davies (1990) found that friends had greater dominance in the companionship than the confidant networks, especially among those who were previously married and whose children lived at a distance. Friends were important in the confidant networks of those who were previously married and childless and those who were married and had no children living close by.

Communication. Among the various activities that Dykstra's (1990) participants reported sharing with their closest network members, several categories of communication received ratings of often or always: 74% stated that they talked about everyday things, 33% discussed their mistakes, 22% revealed their deepest feelings, and 15% talked about the quality of the relationship.

Conflict. Disagreements and disappointments occur in older-adult friendships as well as in friendships of younger persons. Dykstra (1990) reported on two aspects of conflict: whereas 38% of respondents disagreed with the statement that they never argued with close network members, only 22% agreed that a friend sometimes upset them. Fisher, Reid, and Melendez (1989) probed into the causes of anger with friends. Older adults revealed that they became angry at friends who failed to live up to role expectations for older adults (i.e., adapting to the aging process and aging successfully). Another source of conflict was envy over financial matters, health, physical attractiveness, and social relationships.

Social support. As they have done with other age groups, researchers have studied social exchanges and social support in late adult friendships. Shea et al. (1988) investigated exchange of resources (affection, esteem, information, and services) in old and new friendships of older adults. Longstanding close friendships were characterized by stability of resource exchange, whereas relationships that developed from acquaintanceship to friendship evidenced increases in frequency of resource exchange. Roberto and Scott (1986a) reported that more than half their respondents had equitable exchanges with their best friends. Those who had inequitable relationships claimed more distress associated with the friendship than those with equitable exchanges.

Social support is typically studied as a network process, although the source of data is usually the individual respondent, not the network. Roberto and Scott (1984-85) found that widowed elderly women received more help from friends than married women received. Bossé, Aldwin, Levenson, Workman-Daniels, and Ekerdt (1990) compared older male workers and retirees. Although 43% of the sample members had talked with a friend from work about a problem in the last three months, in general, only small proportions of respondents used coworkers as confidants. Retirees reported less quantitative support (i.e., size of network and frequency of interaction) than workers, but retirees and workers did not differ on quality of support (i.e., number of confidants and someone to rely on in emergencies).

Betrayal. Hansson, Jones, and Fletcher (1990) noted that besides providing social support, networks can be sources of mixed motives, competition for scarce resources, plotting, deception, and violations of trust. In their study most of the accounts of betrayal described situations that had taken place decades ago. Same-sex friends were betrayed by 16.7% of respondents; only spouses were betrayed by a larger proportion (25%). Spouses and coworkers were more common sources of betrayal than friends (55.6%, 19.4%, and 8.3% respectively). Respondents were more likely to attribute their betrayal of others to external motivations and unintentional factors than was the case for others' betrayal of them. Also fewer respondents believed that their act of betrayal had harmed the relationship than believed that another's betrayal of them had damaged the relationship. Positive correlations were found between having betrayed a higher proportion of network members and being betrayed by a higher proportion, regretting more relationships, and experiencing more conflict in the network. Those who felt betrayed by a high proportion of network members depended on fewer members and regretted more of their relationships. These findings paralleled similar research on younger adults.

Proxy Measures of Process

Quantity of interaction. Length of acquaintance varies across levels of solidarity in older adults' friendships as in younger adults' friendships. Best and closest friends had been known for 23 to 39 years, whereas length of less close friendships ranged from 19 to 24 years (Adams, 1985-1986; Blieszner, 1982; Jones & Vaughan, 1990; Roberto & Scott, 1984-1985). The long-term friendships in Shea et al. (1988) were 5 to 70 years in length; the new friendships were just 4 months old. In Cohen and Rajkowski's (1982) sample of hotel residents, respondents had known their friends and their nonfriend contacts for averages of 17 and 5 years, respectively.

Reported frequency of interaction among older adult friends varied from an average of several times a month (Adams, 1985-1986; Blieszner, 1982) to weekly (Dykstra, 1990; Jones & Vaughan, 1990) or daily, depending on marital status (Roberto & Scott, 1984-1985). Blieszner (1982) further reported that respondents had significantly longer in-person or telephone visits with their closest friends (2 to 4 hours on average) than with casual friends or acquaintances (averaging 2 hours or less).

Variety of processes. We found no studies that directly addressed multiplexity in the friendships of older adults. Reports of social support and shared activities (e.g., Bossé et al., 1990; Cohen, 1989; Connidis & Davies, 1990; Roberto & Scott, 1986a, 1986b; Rook, 1987) provide indirect evidence that many older adults are involved in multiplex relationships. They receive several varieties of support from their friends, and they enjoy diverse activities together. The availability of social support and companionship enhances older adults' subjective well-being. But at present it is not possible to answer questions such as how many different roles do older adults share with friends at various levels of solidarity?

Data on directionality in older adults' friendships are available in Blieszner (1982, in press) and Goodman (1985). Respondents in the former study reported that they received resources slightly less often than they gave them, whereas those in the latter study claimed reciprocal relationships. It appears that healthy older adults maintain a balance of giving and receiving in their friendships.

⁊ Gender and the Life Course

Analysis of friendship processes across genders and over the life course is even more sparse than for the particular groups of adults discussed above. We found comparative evidence for cognitive and behavioral, but not affective, processes and for limited proxy measures.

Cognitive Processes

Conceptions of friendship. The meaning of friendship seems to vary across age groups in adulthood. Tesch and Martin (1983) compared friendship conceptions of college students and young adult alumni, about 5 years older than the students. Respondents emphasized reciprocity as an important value of friendship, including dependability, caring, commitment, and trust as key elements. The older respondents, however, were less likely to mention trust, understanding, confiding, ego support, and respect than the younger. They were more likely than the younger group to mention acknowledgement of differences between partners and ease of communication. There were no sex differences in these results.

Another study involved participants in describing characteristics of ideal and real friends. Weiss and Lowenthal (1975) found that the descriptions of real friends were similar among members of the four life stages represented in the sample, suggesting that the functions of friends may be established early in life and remain fairly constant throughout. With respect to ideal friends, similarity was important to high school seniors but decreased in importance across the three older groups, reflecting teenagers' concern with identity formation. The discrepancy between attributes of real and ideal friends decreased from high school to newlywed to middle-aged respondents, but was high for older adults. This finding may reflect increasing selectivity of friends as people mature to middleage, but greater concern about interpersonal relations in the later years. Weiss and Lowenthal (1975) found greater sex differences than life stage differences in friend qualities. Women provided more detailed descriptions of real and ideal friend attributes than men gave. Men emphasized similarity, and women focused on reciprocity across all four stages. The oldest group of participants gave more complex descriptions of friendship than the teenagers; the middle-aged persons had the simplest descriptions, perhaps because of family demands that competed with friendship.

In a study of characteristics of best friends, Goldman, Cooper, Ahern, and Corsini (1981) surveyed women in six age groups. Junior high and elderly women used significantly fewer categories than those in senior high or those in their 20s and 30s. The attributes "common interests and activities" and "friend as giver" were important to respondents of all ages, with intimacy also important up through middle-aged respondents. These results are comparable to the Weiss and Lowenthal (1975) findings for similarity and reciprocity. The differences in important friend attributes across age groups reflected the stage of personal and family development of members in each group.

Affective Processes

We found no studies that included simultaneous comparisons of affective processes across genders and stages of the life course. Obviously this suggests the need for comparative investigations on how women and men and people at different points in life are similar or different in the feelings associated with friendship.

Behavioral Processes

Expressions of affection. The manner of demonstrating feelings of closeness did not vary across the life stages represented in Stueve and Gerson's (1977) sample, even though frequency of contact did. When the investigators controlled for length of acquaintance, however, they found that older men were somewhat less likely than younger men to rate their longterm friendships as very close. Perhaps this was because the younger men's longterm friendships were childhood friendships. For all life-stage groups, the earlier the person had met his best friend, the more intimate the friendship.

Intimacy can be assessed in terms of empathy, altruism, and companionship, as Fox et al. (1985) did among people aged 18 to 75. Across all age groups men were less expressive in their friendships than were women. Men talked about sports, politics, and business, whereas women discussed feelings and problems with their friends. Middle-aged and older people expressed deeper and more complex ideas about friendship and made more efforts to reduce disagreements with their friends than did the younger respondents.

Communication. Dickson-Markman (1986) investigated self-disclosure with friends, focusing on the life course. She found that four age groups of adults ranging from 19 to 91 years old were more similar than different on various dimensions of self-disclosure when length of friendship was taken into account. The only age-group difference that occurred was that the negative valence of self-disclosure was higher for older respondents than for younger ones.

Proxy Measures of Process

Quantity of interaction. Average length of acquaintance with same-sex friends varied by age of respondent from 7 to 29 years (Dickson-Markman, 1986; Stueve & Gerson, 1977). Stueve and Gerson (1977) concluded that men under age 35 shift their best friends fairly often, but men older than 35 retain theirs.

With regard to frequency of contact, Stueve and Gerson (1977) and Farrell and Rosenberg (1981) found that young single men and middle-aged men saw their friends more often than did young married men. Both sets of authors interpreted these results in terms of family responsibilities that increased across the years from young to middle adulthood, taking time from friendship, but decreased again for men in the launching phase of the family cycle, leaving more time for activities with friends.

Variety of processes. Both middle-aged and older adults thought that the majority of their exchanges were reciprocal, although relationships with friends and children were somewhat less reciprocal than those with spouses (Ingersoll-Dayton & Antonucci, 1988). The direction of perceived nonreciprocity was instrumental; respondents believed that they gave more support than they received. Although older adults were more likely than middle-aged ones to receive support from family members that they would not be able to reciprocate, there were no age differences in nonreciprocated support received from friends.

❧ Summary and Research Implications

The literature contains scattered studies of various cognitive, affective, and behavioral processes in adult friendship but no systematic analyses of a comprehensive array of processes. Self-disclosure and social support, two behavioral processes, appear to be the most commonly studied types of interaction. Most of the research has been conducted with college students; only a small number of reports on processes among older adults, and even fewer on middle-aged adults, have appeared. Many of the existing studies (not reviewed in this chapter) are laboratory experiments concerned with short-term interactions rather than ongoing friendships. The friendship process literature reflects dyadic interaction but not network relationships or the connections between dyads and networks.

Our conceptual model suggests many questions for new research on process aspects of friendship. For example, in what ways do individuals enact their friendships in everyday life? How do cognitive and affective processes affect friendship enactment? Do women and men differ with respect to cognitive, affective, and behavioral processes of friendship? Do people at various stages of the life course differ on these friendship processes? Do processes change over time and with phases of friendship? Similar questions specific to each cognitive, affective, and behavioral process discussed in this chapter —and others not yet researched—can also be generated. Although certain answers to these questions are available for some groups of adults, a comprehensive understanding of friendship processes over the life course requires samples of multiple age groups and both genders, assessed on the same variables, to permit comparative analyses.

5

Phases of Friendship

Friendship is a dynamic relationship. Its development progresses from acquaintanceship to emotional closeness (and sometimes, discord) through the interactive processes described in Chapter 4. We prefer the term *phases* instead of *stages* to describe friendship transformations because we do not wish to imply that friendship occurs according to a fixed sequence of transitions or results in a fixed relational outcome (see McCall, 1988). Some friendships become very close (high solidarity) and others remain at a casual level (low solidarity); some friendships follow a smooth trajectory of increasing closeness over time and others move back and forth between greater and lesser solidarity; some friendships develop quickly and others evolve slowly. Phases of friendship take place over time; they are not static events.

Although it is difficult to specify the phases of friendship development precisely, for the sake of discussion we address what takes

90

place when friendships are initiated, how they are maintained or changed, and how problems, including dissolution of the friendship, are handled. Individuals bring their positions in the social structure, their developmental histories, and their dispositions to each phase of friendship. Friendship, like other close relationships, thus represents the convergence of individual, societal, and relationship development (see Kimmel, 1979).

In this chapter we present reviews of research on friendship initiation, maintenance, and dissolution in adulthood and then compare results across genders and life stages. Readers should keep in mind the previous discussion of the limitations of published research associated with sampling, definitions of friendship, and methods of study as well as statements about the influence of life course stages on friend relationships.

֎ College Student Friendships

The stage of the life course that has received the most research attention on phases of friendship is young adulthood, represented only by samples of college students. As indicated in Chapter 3, the unique institutional setting of higher education provides unusual opportunities for making friends. Not surprisingly, initiation of friendship is the phase most frequently studied.

Initiation

VanLear and Trujillo (1986) presented a model of social judgment processes that occur as people become acquainted. First is a period of *uncertainty* in which individuals do not know what to expect from each other, so affective reactions, trust, and attraction are low. As partners come to know each other a little more, they move into the *exploration* stage, during which uncertainty decreases and partners become more comfortable together. Next is the *interpersonal growth* stage, when interaction becomes even more positive, with trust and attraction increasing significantly. Finally, partners experience *interpersonal stability* at some level of solidarity—as acquaintances or more intimate friends—depending on how much trust, attraction, and so on evolves. Partners can make the decision about whether or not to develop a friendship very early in the relationship—within the first few hours of meeting—and the friendship can become very close within a few weeks' time (Berg & Clark, 1986).

Communication is the main means by which the acquaintance process unfolds. Miell and Duck (1986) were concerned with the ways individuals controlled the information cues that defined appropriate behavior during the course of friendship development. In the first interactions with a new partner respondents were careful to be polite, not talk about too broad a range of topics, and not reveal too much about themselves. At the same time they tried to discover information about the partner by asking questions and observing the partner's reactions. Based on early conversations, observations, and inferences, those who wanted to restrict the development of the relationship remained polite and talked about general topics but did not continue to ask questions, be responsive, or observe the partner. On the other hand, those who decided to become more involved with the partner began to discuss a wider range of topics than before, at a deeper level, and during more frequent meetings. They made the decision to intensify the friendship based on criteria such as how trustworthy, easy going, easy to talk to, and available the person seemed to be. The subsequent conversations helped to increase trust and understanding, which in turn led to greater closeness. At that point discussion of personal problems and exchanges of advice took place, reflecting the existence of close friendship.

In a series of reports on longitudinal studies, Hays (1984, 1985) described attitudinal and other behavioral changes as partners moved from acquaintanceship to close friendship. The friendships that became closer over time, compared to those that did not, increased in amount and breadth of interaction and moved from fairly superficial to increasingly intimate levels of behavior exchange (see also Baxter & Wilmot, 1986). Thus multiplex relationships seem to be important for friendship development. Despite some decline in interaction frequency, growing friendships were rated increasingly higher on intimacy over time, showing that friendship bonds were more dependent on affection than on frequency of contact. Respondents whose friendships grew, compared to nonfriends, reported more relationship benefits and increasing benefits over time. The two groups did not differ on perceived costs, implying that benefits are more important than costs in friendship development.

In terms of predictors of friendship initiation and development, Berg (1984) conducted a longitudinal study of dyads who began the academic year as unacquainted roommates and ended it by deciding whether or not to live together the following year. Students who chose not to continue living together had decreased in liking and satisfaction with the friendship over time, reported a decrease in help received from their roommates, saw themselves as dissimilar to their roommates, and evaluated their current living arrangement less favorably than alternatives. Like Hays (1984), Berg found that the decision about whether to continue the friendship was made fairly early in the relationship.

At least seven studies of the effects of similarity on college student friendship formation have appeared. Among the types of matching that contribute to initial attraction are similarity of personality (Blankenship, Hnat, Hess, & Brown, 1984; Duck, 1973; Duck & Craig, 1978), attitudes (Baker, 1983; Knapp & Harwood, 1977; Neimeyer & Mitchell, 1988), and values (Lea & Duck, 1982). Once friends are attracted to each other, interaction between them leads to increased similarity because of mutual socialization (Baker, 1983). Consonant with the filtering hypothesis (Duck, 1973), the salience of different domains of similarity may change as acquaintances become friends (Blankenship et al., 1984; Neimeyer & Mitchell, 1988). Cahn (1990) argued, however, that at later stages of relationship development, similarity may become less important than the feeling of being understood.

Maintenance

Once friendships are established, individuals need to nurture them; as noted in Chapter 4, friendships can endure for decades. The label *maintenance* for this middle phase of friendship, however, does not refer only to relationship stability. On the contrary, many changes in individuals, dyads, and networks can occur during this phase;

such changes can strengthen, weaken, or have little effect on friendship bonds. Even disturbing processes such as disagreements and conflict can have beneficial effects on friendship (Braiker & Kelley, 1979; Hirsch, 1980).

One way that partners maintain their friendships, according to Argyle and Henderson (1984), is to follow the normative rules of friendship concerning behavioral exchanges, intimacy, relations with respect to third parties outside the dyad, and coordination of interaction. Of course, the ability to keep the rules depends on both knowing them and possessing the requisite social skills to follow them (e.g., Trower, 1981).

Several researchers found that the strategies used to maintain friendships varied by level of closeness. For example, Argyle and Henderson (1984) observed that some rules were kept more often in close than in casual friendships. Keeping casual friends as opposed to close or best friends required more physical proximity but less affection, whereas retention of close and best friendships required at least some expressed affection and a great deal of interaction (Rose & Serafica, 1986). Hays (1989) also found that, compared to casual friends, close friends interacted more frequently, interacted across a greater range of settings, felt that their interactions were more exclusive and provided more benefits, and weighted costs of friendship less heavily.

Another type of comparison is between friendships that are either stable, becoming closer, or becoming less close. Baxter and Wilmot (1986) found that stable friendships were characterized by lower levels of satisfaction, interaction effectiveness, and interaction personalness than were friendships still growing, and actually were not different on these variables from disengaging relationships—at least during the brief two weeks of the study.

How do people keep friendships stable if they don't want any change in solidarity? Ayres (1983) argued that the answer depends on the person's perception of the partner's goals. Respondents who wanted the relationship to continue at its current level and thought the partner's intentions were the same used a combination of three strategies in their interactions. *Avoidance strategies* involved ignoring things the partner did to change the relationship and not doing things that might change it. *Balance* strategies included keeping favors and emotional support levels constant. *Directness* strategies encompassed telling the partner that one wants the relationship to remain as it is. In contrast, respondents who perceived that the partner wanted to develop the relationship used avoidance and directness to keep it stable. Finally, those who believed that the partner wanted the relationship to *deteriorate* focused on balance strategies in an effort to keep the friendship going.

What factors contribute to the endurance of closeness over time? Griffin and Sparks (1990) were better able to predict male-male closeness after 4 years than female-female closeness. Significant predictors of male-male friendship closeness as measured at the beginning of the study were perceived status similarity, shared knowledge, being roommates, and fewer taboo topics of conversation. Another important predictor was geographic distance after 4 years, with those living closer together being emotionally closer as well. Overall, similarity seemed to be important for continued closeness, at least for male friends.

In summary, the ways people sustain friendship usually revolve around continued similarity, rewarding communication and interaction patterns, and positive feelings. Wright (1984) noted, however, that some friendships endure even though one or both partners may no longer find the relationship rewarding. According to Wright's self-referent model of friendship, this result occurs because continuation of a nonrewarding friendship contributes to the individual's positive self-image as a caring and loyal person. Wright implied that nonrewarding friendships are affectively neutral; overtly negative friendships, characterized by stable but unpleasant interactions, also exist. Neimeyer and Neimeyer (1985) suggested that negative relationships may endure because each partner can contrast her or his traits or behavior with the undesirable ones in the partner, thus indirectly validating the self-image.

Dissolution

Argyle and Henderson (1984) found that friendships fell apart when one of the partners violated general rules of friendship such as keeping confidences and not criticizing one's friend in public. Lack of social skills, inappropriate forms of self-disclosure, inability to express feelings, failure to conform to resource exchange expectations (Duck, 1981), and having less time to spend together because one of the partners established a romantic relationship (Rose, 1984) are other causes of friendship decline. Also a friendship might lapse if either partner's criteria for what they like in a friend change or if a friend changes in directions that lead to display of traits or behaviors that the partner dislikes (Hays, 1988; Rose, 1984).

College students invoke different ways of terminating friendship. According to Argyle and Henderson (1984), relationship rules operate to structure the disengagement process when friendship lapses. At such a time partners uphold general informal social rules but not specific friendship rules about intimacy and support, thus maintaining the social norm of commitment to the ideal of a relationship despite lack of closeness. In Rose's (1984) study some students ended friendships via physical separation, such as failing to exchange addresses when one partner moved away. Others simply replaced old friends with new ones, often under amiable circumstances. Individuals tended to be less direct in disengaging from friendships than from romantic liaisons (Baxter, 1985).

We found no studies of predictors of friendship dissolution per se. Although it may seem intuitively plausible that variables associated with deterioration are the opposites of characteristics associated with initiation and maintenance of friendship, this is not necessarily the case. For example, expressions of affection are important to starting friendship and keeping it going, but a decline in affect does not necessarily result in the desire to end a relationship (Duck, 1981). Thus researchers should investigate specifically the causes of deterioration and dissolution in friendships of young adults.

❧ Adult Friendships

As discussed in Chapter 3, friendship phases in the adult years are affected by the differential opportunities of adults, compared to college students, to meet potential friends and promote friendships.

Differences in developmental maturity and roles may affect their reasons and strategies for friendship dissolution. Unfortunately the literature on phases of friendship in adulthood is extremely limited. Although there are studies of the middle years of adulthood that include descriptions of desired characteristics of friends, activities with friends, and other data implying that individuals strive to build and sustain friendships during these years, we found few studies that explicitly asked middle-aged persons about the strategies they used to do so. This is a critical oversight, especially in light of the stress and coping literature that shows the importance of support from friends for dealing with critical life events. Given the major life review and evaluation processes that begin in the middle years, it seems crucial to understand the connection between the need for social support and friendship patterns at this stage of the life cycle.

Initiation

One source of friendship in the middle years is groups in which the individual holds membership. Stein (1986) described the evolution of friendship in men's consciousness-raising groups. These friendships developed slowly, based on shared trust, exchange of information, and a growing sense of commitment between partners. Lack of time to get together and feelings of competitiveness, greater achievement drives, and fears of getting too close were obstacles to friendship initiation.

Maintenance

Communication strategies are important in friendship mainte-nance. Rawlins (1983a, 1983b) analyzed the dialectical interplay be-tween independence and dependence in friendship and between the expressive and protective functions of communication in friendship. On the one hand, the contradictory opportunities of autonomy to pursue individual goals or interests and interdependence in times of need require ongoing negotiations between friends to keep the privileges of friendship in balance. On the other hand, friends must also balance expressiveness (self-disclosure, directness, honesty, candor) with protectiveness (avoiding hurtful remarks or touchy subjects). Successful management of these communication dilemmas contributes to the maintenance of friendship.

Turning from strategies to predictors of adult friendship maintenance, Suitor (1987) examined changes in interaction with friends of women who enrolled in college. Of course full-time students had less time to interact with friends, but relationships with less-educated friends were more difficult to maintain than those with their better-educated friends because the former group did not approve of the return to school. Part-time students, on the other hand, maintained friendships with their less-educated friends even as friendships with their better-educated friends declined. The explanation is that the status of student was less central to the identity of the part-time students, so they were better able than the full-time students to tolerate their friends' negative attitudes about the return to school.

Dissolution

No studies of adult dissolution strategies and just one on predictors of dissolution were found. In an analysis of discussion group partners over the course of 20 weeks, Neimeyer and Neimeyer (1986) discovered that in dyads that did not become close, at least one partner's level of attraction decreased over time, whereas in dyads that grew closer, the average level of attraction increased over time. The deteriorating dyad members were low on functional similarity to begin with and showed less similarity in their construction of social reality over time, but increased on functional similarity from the first to the second measurement. The authors concluded that consensual validation is important during the formative stage of the acquaintance process because lack of it early in the interactions impeded friendship development.

⋆ Old Age Friendships

The literature contains many studies of social support and other functions of friendship in old age. Thus there is plenty of evidence that friendships do exist to the end of the life cycle. In contrast, there is little research on friendship phases in late adulthood.

Initiation

Several studies of friendship initiation are available. First, we have indirect evidence suggesting that friendship formation occurs throughout life. Matthews (1986) identified, by means of retrospective interviews, three styles of friendship behavior reflecting patterns that had emerged over the respondents' lives. Members of the group she termed *acquisitive* were more likely than others to continue to make new friends in the later years. These individuals reported that their friend networks increased in size as they experienced life events such as job changes, relocation, or changes in marital status.

Direct evidence about friendship initiation in old age appears in articles by Blieszner (1989b) and Shea et al. (1988). The authors investigated friendship development among strangers who moved into a newly constructed retirement community at the same time. Within 5 months of becoming acquainted, respondents differentiated among their old and new friends on both subjective and behavioral measures. They reported more liking, loving, and commitment for friends who grew closer than for those who became less close. At the beginning of the study old friends, acquaintances who eventually became friends, and acquaintances who did not become friends did not differ on the perceived likelihood or actual frequency of exchanging resources; but 5 months later old friends and those who became closer received higher scores on the likelihood and frequency of exchange measures than did friends who became more distant. Thus both affective and behavioral variables are important contributors to the evolution of new friendships in old age.

Maintenance

Several researchers have looked at friend-retention strategies of older adults. For example, Matthews (1986) found that some friendships endured due to favorable social circumstances such as visits to the home town or school reunions rather than to respondents' explicit efforts to maintain them. Other friendships continued over time because the partners engaged in letter writing, telephoning, and visiting, or they selected a retirement community near their friends or went on vacations together. These more active versus rather passive styles of friendship maintenance seemed to be linked both to individual personality characteristics and to lifelong friend interaction styles.

Elderly people may use different maintenance strategies for old than for new friends (Blieszner, 1989b; Shea et al., 1988). Respondents took expressions of affection as givens in old friendships, whereas new ones required displays of affection to aid in their growth and maintenance. Conveying esteem for each other was crucial for both ongoing and fairly new friends. Respondents valued advice from their old friends and engaged in reminiscing and self-disclosure with them, but the information they shared with new friends focused more on current day-to-day events and less personal topics. Old friends exchanged various forms of services and assistance as needed, and study participants appreciated the help and support that old friends had provided over the years. Exchange of services was not, however, a significant part of relationship maintenance between new friends, and those who did do favors for each other had a concern about reciprocity that was not evident in the discussions of old friendships.

By studying a unique population, Elder and Clipp (1988) uncovered other influences on friendship maintenance. They examined social bonding among old male veterans of the Armed Forces. Having shared intense combat experiences and losses of comrades, veterans retained strong ties to service friends because "the act of remembering a life period or event maintains contact with people who were important at the time. Such memories perpetuate social bonds and are, in turn, sustained by them" (p. 193). Such ties can serve a very beneficial purpose by helping veterans overcome the long-term stresses associated with combat experience.

Friend networks not only endure throughout life, they also can change in old age just as at any other stage. Adams (1987) observed this in a 3-year investigation of older women and their networks. When study participants had been freed from the constraints on their friendships imposed by obligations to family, community, and work during middle age, they became liberated from their old patterns and developed different networks.

Dissolution

In both Matthews's (1986) and Blieszner's (1989b) research on older adult friendships, it appeared that friendships just "faded away" due to diverging life-styles and pathways over the years; few individuals actively terminated friendships. Some friendships deteriorated because one of the partners became ill (see Johnson, 1983) or moved away. Because these friendships had not ended in disharmony, respondents felt they could revitalize them if circumstances should permit—unlike the assumption of a permanent rift that younger adults tend to hold when a friendship disintegrates.

❧ Gender and the Life Course

In this section we summarize the handful of studies in which researchers made comparisons across stages of the life course and genders regarding the initiation and maintenance phases. We have no examples of research on the dissolution phase, however.

Initiation

Young adult women and men show many similarities and some differences in preferred strategies for initiating friendships. According to Rose (1985), in a comparison of college students and college graduates about 3 years older, both women and men agreed on strategies important for beginning same-sex friendships. These included proximity, acceptance, effort, communication, common interests, and affection. In contrast, time and sexual attraction were significantly more often viewed as ways of forming cross-sex than same-sex friendships. Nevertheless, respondents expressed unwillingness, lack of interest, and difficulty in forming and maintaining cross-sex friendships. Women were not motivated by sexual attraction to start such relationships, but men were. Being married, more than age, inhibited the development of cross-sex friendships. Although life stage differences occurred on a few of the strategies of forming same- and cross-sex friendships, for the most part the students and graduates agreed on the patterns given above.

A comparison of young adult and middle-aged men revealed some life stage differences in predictors of friendship initiation. Wall, Pickert, and Paradise (1984) reported that married and separated or divorced men, regardless of age, emphasized the importance of current activities at work and in the neighborhood for initiating friendship. Single men in both age groups, however, were more likely to mention personality traits as the chief facilitator of friendship formation. Regarding inhibitors of friendship initiation, Wall and associates found that the greatest constraint for older men, regardless of marital status, was lack of time; younger married men echoed this opinion. For younger unmarried respondents, personality characteristics were inhibiting factors in friendship formation. It appears that younger men have a greater concern about personality issues in friendship than older ones.

Maintenance

Do the rules of friendship maintenance differ across age groups? Argyle and Henderson (1984) hypothesized an affirmative answer, such that rules endorsed by younger adults would emphasize help and availability more than those endorsed by middle-aged adults. This hypothesis was not confirmed by the data, in which the two age groups of respondents did not differ in the rules they emphasized. In a separate study of young adults from ages 17 to 34 years, older respondents were more likely to attribute the end of a friendship to lack of respect for privacy and too many requests for personal advice, whereas younger participants were more likely to attribute it to public criticism.

Some of the strategies that contribute to retention of friendships vary for women and men and for same- and cross-sex friendships, but not for students and recent graduates (Rose, 1985). Both women and men endorsed strategies related to acceptance, effort, time, communication, common interests, and affection as important for same-sex friendship maintenance. Women, more often than men, reported having no strategy for keeping cross-sex friendships. Also women were less likely than men to view time as important in sustaining cross-sex friendships.

✿ Summary and Research Implications

As pointed out by Baxter and Wilmot (1986), most friendship research has been grounded in a conceptualization of friendship as a static state of individuals rather than as a potentially changing relationship. Thus we found the smallest number of studies to illustrate the friendship phases part of our model as compared to the structure and process components.

The majority of friendship phase researchers have examined the initiation phase. Given that the studies were based on college students or, in the case of one investigation of older adults, new residents of a retirement community—both situations that present a highly structured set of opportunities for meeting people—the perspective on how people form new friendships in adulthood is actually rather limited. Data on how nonstudent young adults, middle-aged adults, or older adults living in the regular community manage to make new friends are nonexistent, so whether the same mechanisms operate for them as for college students is unknown.

Longitudinal studies of transitions from one phase to another are quite rare as are studies of friendship maintenance and dissolution. We found no studies of network phases, thus it is impossible to determine whether dyadic phases affect network phases and vice versa. All of these issues suggest the need for additional research on friendship phases within the context of the friendship model proposed in this book.

✿ Conclusion: The Interface of Structure, Processes, and Phases

Figure 1.1 illustrated a model of friendship that emphasized the interconnectedness of structure, processes, and phases in describing friendship patterns. We have organized the literature reviews in Chapters 3, 4, and 5 to provide examples of research on these three components of friendship patterns. Implicit in some reports, but not all by any means, are the implications of the other two components for the one under study. In order to make the implicit connections explicit, we would need to review research in which structure, processes, and phases were examined conjointly. Although a few studies on the interplay of structure and process exist (e.g., Hobfoll & Stokes, 1988, and Hirsch, 1980, on network density and social support), there are insufficient studies to flesh out a discussion at this point. Thus we advocate research that integrates the elements of the model displayed in Figure 1.1.

This interconnected set of features both underlies and perpetuates friendship; but friendships are not always initiated and enacted smoothly. In the following chapter we discuss programs and ideas that might be applied to various levels of intervention with the goal of improving friendship.

6

Adult Friendship Intervention

People attempt to change and manipulate social lives—both their own and other people's—every day. People join clubs and organizations to make new acquaintances. Therapists help their clients develop interpersonal skills. Architects create environments to enhance social interaction. Consultants advise companies on how to create amiable work milieus. Planners design communities to facilitate contact among residents. Policymakers pass laws that encourage people to rely on their friends and relatives for help rather than on formal agencies.

Although the people who initiate and implement these efforts might not think of them as interventions, they in fact are. The word *intervention* is not totally satisfactory, because it implies some noble, selfless, or at least socially acceptable goal. Sometimes, however, social interventions are designed for profit. For example, someone might join a country club to develop relationships with people who could be helpful in business. An organization might manipulate informal relationships in an effort to raise productivity. A government might advocate dependency on others in lieu of supporting service programs with tax dollars.

Some relationship interventions are informed by systematic research on social interaction. But although altering friendship patterns is often the goal of many interventions, few are based on a familiarity with the specific literature on friendship. Perhaps this is because the friendship research literature is not yet coherent and comprehensive (see Chapter 1). Perhaps it is because friendship researchers have not usually specified the possible applications of their findings. Or perhaps it is because friendship is considered a voluntary and somewhat sacred relationship, and, therefore, not an acceptable target for intervention.

Despite ethical or political opinions that friendships should not be consciously manipulated, especially by people other than those involved, social interventions are routinely implemented, often without the knowledge of the participants. The failure to use friendship research findings in developing and executing social interaction interventions is thus unfortunate. A haphazardly conceived intervention is more dangerous than or, at least, less beneficial than no intervention at all.

Although some social intervention principles probably apply equally to all types of relationships, not all do. Friendship, family relationships, neighboring, and acquaintanceship are each characterized by different structures and processes. Furthermore, in each type of relationship, the structures and processes are related to one another in distinctive ways. Interventions intended to alter the patterns of each type of relationship must therefore be somewhat different.

The purpose of this chapter is twofold. First, we want to encourage friendship researchers to consider potential applications of their findings. Even if investigators do not wish to specify the practical implications of their research, they must take responsibility for thinking about how others might apply their findings. Second, we want to prompt practitioners who design social interaction interventions to familiarize themselves with the friendship literature and to apply the findings. Even if the goal is not to manipulate friendship patterns specifically, interventions should at least be designed so that they do not undermine existing relationships.

Figure 6.1 depicts the intervention model discussed in the remainder of this book. Interventions affecting friendship patterns can be implemented at various levels (see left panel). If the intervention is successful, the change in friendship patterns results in desirable outcomes (see right panel). An intervention at one level can affect outcomes at the same level which, in turn, affect outcomes at lower levels (see arrows between levels on right panel).

This model resembles Bronfenbrenner's (1986) discussion of the ecology of the family as a context for human development in the sense that both models address the effect of context on outcome, and, specifically, consider the effects of the individual's immediate context (e.g., the family or friendship network) as well as more remote ones (e.g., community). Our model differs in its inclusion of a broader range of intervention levels and a broader range of possible outcomes. Although we discuss our model in terms of friendship intervention, it could easily be adapted for use in interventions with other relationships.

ఆ Outcomes of Friendship Interventions

Why might someone want to change or manipulate friendship patterns? More specifically, why might someone want to change the friendship patterns of an individual, of a pair of friends, in an entire friendship network, in a specific context, in an entire community, or even in an entire society (see right panel of Figure 6.1)? One possible goal of friendship intervention would be to increase individuals' satisfaction with their friendships. Less obvious, perhaps, would be to change their behavior, attitudes, values, situations (e.g., financial, social), or conditions (e.g., health, mental health).

In order to design interventions to effect such changes, information on the types of friendship patterns that predict the desirable outcomes is necessary. We have already discussed the gaps in the literature on friendship patterns themselves (see Chapters 3-5). Although researchers have studied a variety of consequences of

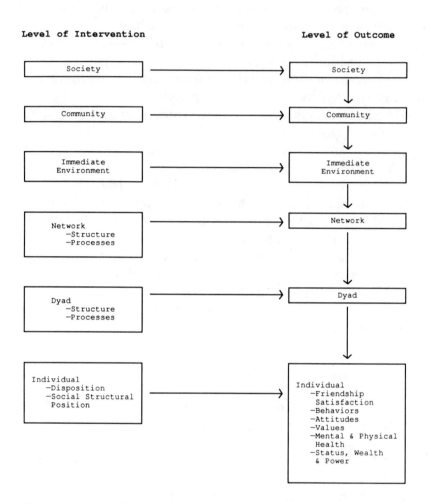

Figure 6.1. Friendship Intervention

friendship for the individual, they have not often studied the consequences of friendship patterns for the dyad, the network, or their contexts.

Investigators have examined some connections between friendship patterns and possible individual-level outcomes more often and more thoroughly than others. They have, for example, repeatedly investigated the relationship between friendship patterns and both social support and psychological well-being (see reviews in Antonucci, 1989; Larson, 1978; Peplau & Perlman, 1982). In contrast, although many people accept the notion that "it is not what you know, but who you know that matters," researchers have not often studied the effects of friendship on status, power, and wealth. This is probably because social relationships are not supposed to be formed and maintained for the purposes of individual gain. Although researchers studying adolescents have examined the influence of friends on attitudes, behavior, and values (e.g., Tokuno, 1986), researchers studying adults have not often addressed these topics. This neglect is probably because most researchers assume that during adulthood identity is more crystallized and people behave and think more autonomously than during adolescence. Until recently researchers had not studied health as an outcome of friendship patterns (see Baron, Cutrona, Hicklin, Russell, & Lubaroff, 1990 for an example and an overview of this literature), probably because understanding of the connections between emotions and physiological response had not been well developed.

ⅈ Levels of Intervention

How does one go about changing friendship patterns? The answer depends the level of the intervention. An intervention at one level would affect friendship patterns at that level and at levels below it (see Figure 6.1). For example, a friendship network intervention would affect the friendship patterns in the network, in the dyads that compose it, and of the individual members. Of course the more remote the level of intervention from the target level, the less successful it is likely to be. To change the friendship patterns of an individual, for example, it would not be efficient or necessarily effective to try to bring about change in community friendship interaction. A lower-level intervention would be more sensible.

Depending on the level at which change is desired, the type of intervention also must vary. To bring about change in the friendship patterns of individuals, one must alter the personality dispositions or structural positions of those individuals—their ways of relating to people or their opportunities to make and maintain friendships. To bring about change in dyadic or network relationships, one must manipulate their structures and processes. At the remaining levels one must create or alter contexts to facilitate the types of friendship patterns desired. Although literature specifically focused on friendship intervention is scarce, other relevant models and resources are available.

Improving the Individual's Cognitive and Social Functioning

Several literatures address ways of intervening into friendship processes, not structure; it would be difficult, if not impossible, to change a person's structural identity. Although people can change social contexts to enhance friendship opportunities (e.g., join a club, change jobs, move to a new neighborhood; see Weiss, 1973), the success of these commonsense tactics has not been examined. Rather, the emphasis has been on dispositional interventions, as suggested by the techniques of clinical psychology and research on loneliness. Whereas some scholars and therapists advocate helping people change the way they think about themselves and their partners, others focus on social skills development or enhancement.

Cognitive processes. Self-defeating thought processes can interfere with the ability to engage in satisfying close relationships. According to Young (1986), friendship disorders result from stable and enduring patterns of thinking that originate early in life and affect future expectations about relationships. The biased schema lead to problems in initiating or deepening friendships. Common causes of difficulties at the initiation phase are social anxiety, lack of confidence in one's conversational ability, and inadequate awareness of how one's behavior affects others. Problems associated with deepening friendships include not knowing how to pace the relationship, holding unrealistic expectations for friendship, and fear of being entrapped by the demands of others. Other problems apply to both of these phases of friendship: belief that one is unworthy and unlovable, feeling different and alienated, and lack of trust.

Cognitive therapists place emphasis on the connection between thoughts and beliefs on the one hand and feelings and behaviors on the other (Berscheid, Gangestad, & Kulakowski, 1984; Young, 1986). Intervention thus centers on identifying irrational beliefs and sources of inappropriate schema; analyzing the emotional and behavioral outcomes of holding those beliefs and schema; and replacing them with more realistic, accurate, and positive ways of thinking about the self, others, and relationships.

In another approach to cognitive aspects of friendship problems, Tognoli (1980) suggested that men are alienated from other men by homophobia, competition, and cultural proscriptions against expressing feelings or seeking help from others. Men who wish to overcome such alienation must actively defy culturally constrained thinking and acquire more flexible attitudes about the acceptability of expressing affection, vulnerability, and other needs.

Research on expectations regarding friendship also contains suggestions for cognitive interventions. For example, some elderly adults in Matthews's (1983) study believed that it was impossible to replace any of their friends whom they might lose, so they faced a diminishing friendship network in the future. On the other hand, others had a more flexible orientation that allowed them to acquire new friends throughout life. The implication of this distinction is that people in the former category should be helped to expand their thinking so that they are able to maintain a network of friends over time by adding new members to it.

Investigation of communal versus exchange orientations in friendships of college students (Clark et al., 1989) and older adults (Jones & Vaughan, 1990) also has applied implications. The finding that a communal orientation is associated with friendship satisfaction suggests that individuals with an exchange perspective should be helped to focus less on the exact comparability of exchanges and benefits and to think instead about the welfare of their friends.

Social skills. The literature on behavioral interventions with lonely individuals is instructive here. According to Rook's (1984) review, lonely college students, as compared to nonlonely ones, have greater difficulty initiating social contact by introducing themselves to others, making phone calls, and joining groups. They also enjoy themselves less at parties, take fewer social risks, and assert themselves less effectively. They are lower on communication skills such as self-disclosure and responsiveness to others. To counteract these tendencies, counselors use techniques such as modeling, role playing, performance feedback, and homework assignments. Once clients strengthen their friendship initiation skills, they may need further training on how to handle the transition to deeper intimacy.

Ongoing intimate relationships often involve conflict (Braiker & Kelley, 1979). For example, studies of older adults show that jealousy and failure to live up to role expectations are causes of anger among friends (Fisher et al., 1989). Although conflict and negativity are not experienced very often with best friends, when they do occur they diminish satisfaction with the friendship (Jones & Vaughan, 1990). Some adults might be well advised to avoid situations with friends that cause them distress (Fisher et al., 1989), but others would be better served by learning conflict-management strategies (Jones & Vaughan, 1990).

One domain of counseling touches specifically on communication skills as applied both in social and personal relationships and in business arenas. People might be more successful in interactions with friends and others if they learn to use persuasion and compliance-gaining techniques effectively (O'Keefe, 1990), acquire bargaining skills (Winkler, 1981), and develop expertise in negotiation (Raiffa, 1982).

Enhancing Dyadic Interaction

Friendship interventions at the dyadic level focus on changing the partners' behaviors. Marital therapists offer insights about interventions at this level. Although some problems experienced by married couples are not relevant to friendship, others are—especially those that stem from communication difficulties. An example of a dyadic intervention that could be generalized to friend partners is Harrell and Guerney's (1976) program for training married couples in conflict negotiation skills. Other useful skills in friendship are expressiveness, assertiveness, empathy, and promoting change in the self and the partner (Epstein, 1981; Guerney, Brock, & Coufal, 1986).

Marital therapists also emphasize the importance of maintaining a balance between individuality, or differentiation of the self from others, and togetherness, or emotional connectedness, in close relationships (Kerr & Bowen, 1988). Whereas emotional involvement is important to the development and sustenance of friendship (see Chapters 4 and 5), it is equally important that partners maintain a degree of autonomy or self-determination rather than responding to each other only on-the basis of anxiety or other forms of emotional reactivity. From this perspective problems in a friendship would be approached by helping the partners to identify and reduce causes of anxiety and enhance their ability to function autonomously so they can respond to each other in a more adaptive fashion.

Altering Social Relationships in Networks

Gottlieb (1988) argued that intervention at the network level is more ecologically valid than at the individual level for two reasons. First, it is difficult to change basic personality attributes and second, individual-level interventions that conflict with the values and norms of the person's network will be neutralized or discredited by network members. Also, network-level interventions appeal to societal norms of self-reliance, collective action, and empowerment.

One of the most important functions of friend networks is provision of social support via the flow of resources such as tangible aid, companionship, and emotional support through the network (Gottlieb, 1988). Both the provision and the receipt of assistance contribute to feelings of social integration and psychological well-being, although Blieszner (1982) and Goodman (1985) found that giving contributed more to life satisfaction and emotional closeness than receiving. In any case, it is important to find ways to enhance the support provided by existing ties (Thompson & Heller, 1990).

Network interventions theoretically can optimize support by teaching members additional supportive behaviors, changing the structural characteristics of the network, or changing the relationship between the person in need and other members of the network (Gottlieb, 1988). Recent attempts to restructure existing networks and interactions among their members have not been successful, however, and additional research on the connections between network structure and processes is needed before further intervention recommendations can be developed (Gottlieb, 1988).

Educational programs, self-help groups, and informal support groups can supplement naturally occurring friend networks by both helping with relationship or other problems and by providing opportunities to develop new friendships. Research is needed on how the properties of such groups affect their functioning and on the effectiveness of these types of programs for addressing friendship problems (Gottlieb, 1988; Rook, 1984).

The literature on family and group therapy can be consulted for ideas about the conduct of interventions in friend networks. Readers should note, however, that this literature focuses on bounded groups, whereas friend networks are open. Thus we are providing suggestions about the techniques that might be *adapted* for friend networks, rather than claiming that the therapeutic strategies are directly transferable.

Group techniques could be applied to friendship in two ways. The first involves helping a person overcome social skills deficits in a group setting, thus enabling the participant to function more effectively among her or his own friends. Many theoretical frameworks inform the strategies that are used to accomplish such a goal (Gurman & Kniskern, 1981). The second category of group techniques utilizes multiple members of an existing network in a therapeutic intervention scheme. Again, a variety of strategies is available (Gurman & Kniskern, 1981). For example, the procedure described by Rueveni (1979) that brings network members to the counseling session to help individuals and families resolve crises is also applicable to serious friendship problems.

Manipulating Relationships in an
Immediate Environment

An immediate environment is the social and physical context that surrounds individuals and thus structures their interaction with others—for example, a work place, an apartment building, a church, a dormitory, a recreation center, or a nursing home. Depending on her or his gender, stage of life, or other characteristics, a given individual might interact with people in a variety of such environments or in only one. Scholars from many fields, including interior design and architecture, organizational sociology, environmental and industrial psychology, and cultural anthropology, have examined the ways in which immediate environments shape social interaction.

Both the social and physical characteristics of the immediate environment shape the social interaction that occurs within it. An understanding of the effects of both is crucial to designing friendship interventions at this level. Although many authors of ethnographic case studies have described ways in which the characteristics of an immediate social environment (e.g., the status hierarchy, differentiation into cliques, or demographic composition) affect the friendship patterns that develop within it, very few researchers have done systematic studies on this topic. One exception is a study of the effects of the proportion of all residents in an apartment building who were old (age density) on the friendship patterns of older residents. Among other findings Rosow (1967) reported that within both the working and the middle class, the average number of friends increased steadily with rising age density. Furthermore, the higher the age density, the less likely older residents were to seek out or to accept younger friends.

Building on the pioneering work of Hall (1966) and Sommer (1969), Lang (1987) recently wrote an impressive synthesis of the information available on the connection between environmental design and human behavior. An issue that pervades this area of inquiry is competing needs for social interaction and privacy. Early studies by Osmond (1966) showed that some spaces bring people together, facilitating interaction, and others force them apart, inhibiting interaction. Although opportunities for interaction enable people to become acquainted (which is the first step toward friendship), opportunities for privacy (Westin, 1970) are important to the further development of friendship. Social interaction occurs more easily when the opportunities for contact with others are balanced by opportunities for privacy (Lang, 1987). Ambiguous spaces, those that are neither public nor private, discourage social interaction of any type (Flaschbart, 1969).

Most researchers have emphasized the need for built environments that facilitate social interaction rather than the need for those that allow for privacy (e.g., Lawton, 1975; Yancy, 1976). Both functional distance (the degree of difficulty encountered in moving from one point to another) and functional centrality (the ease of access to and frequency of use of common facilities) affect opportunities for social interaction (Lang, 1987). In a classic study of Westgate Housing at the Massachusetts Institute of Technology, Festinger, Schacter, and Back (1950) demonstrated the influence of layout of the environment on contacts among people. On both floors of the residence functional distance was short, but on each floor functional centrality was different. On one floor residents had mailboxes located together and common entrances. On the other they had mailboxes in different locations and entrances from the outside. Contact was much higher on the former floor.

Researchers need to conduct further studies before totally effective friendship interventions can be designed at the level of the immediate environment. Affording people the opportunity to interact with those of similar status is certainly the first step toward facilitating friendship. Allowing people both privacy from those with whom they engage in public interactions and opportunities for developing intimate relationships is certainly another step. Building friendship is, however, more complex than this, and the same friendship patterns are not desirable for everyone. Furthermore, a given individual interacts with others in many environments. Research is thus necessary to examine the effects on friendship patterns of all the characteristics of all the environments in which each individual interacts.

Designing Communities to
Facilitate Social Relationships

The term *community* refers to a group of people who are connected to one another, to some degree, by a web of interpersonal relationships. Community is often used interchangeably with the term *neighborhood*, which refers to a geographic area (Lang, 1987). This discussion of friendship interventions focuses on communities that are also neighborhoods. We will not discuss the possibility of interventions into the friendships among members of nonterritorial communities (Webber, 1970), such as computer bulletin boards or academic professional associations, because too little information is available on them.

The community-organizing, community sociology, ecological psychology, and community-planning literatures are relevant for planning interventions at the community level. The community-organizing literature describes the processes and politics necessary to bring about change in a community (Cox, Erlich, Rothman, & Tropman, 1987). We did not find any discussions of how to bring about changes in friendship patterns. Perhaps this is because community organizing is conceptualized as a problem-solving process (Lowy, 1985), and unsatisfactory friend relations are not typically viewed as problematic in the same way that poverty, poor health, and crime are. Social workers do discuss the building of support networks, especially for the elderly, with the community as client (Biegel, Shore, & Gordon, 1984; Goodman, 1985). By such networks they generally mean connecting people with volunteers and service providers who reduce people's social isolation, give them emotional support, communicate with them, and provide them with instrumental services. These helpers essentially alleviate some of the individual clients' need for friends, but they do not necessarily become friends with the clients. The usefulness of this literature, then, is limited to the general information on the methods of bringing about change.

The community sociology and ecological psychology literatures are useful for identifying variables that might be manipulated to change friendship patterns in an existing community or to establish the desired friendship patterns in a new community. Ecological psychologists have examined the effect of community size on participation (Lang, 1987; Wicker, 1979). The basic premise of these studies is that when there are fewer people in a setting than are necessary for its optimal functioning, people are coerced into greater participation. Smaller settings thus have a higher proportion of people participating and filling roles they would otherwise leave for specialists (Barker & Wright, 1955; Wicker, 1979). The implication is, of course, that because of the higher participation in small communities, friendships will flourish more in them.

In the 1960s community sociologists debated whether propinquity or homogeneity of community was a more important predictor of friend relations. The studies of wartime housing projects and postwar suburban neighborhoods showed that both were important, but homogeneity was more so (Gans, 1976). Gans concluded that propinquity leads to social interaction, but homogeneity is necessary to maintain relationships on a positive basis. He suggested that site planners should not put dwelling units so close together that people are forced to interact with one another or so far apart that visual contact is impossible. Furthermore, blocks should have somewhat homogeneous occupants to promote friendship, but not so homogeneous that any amount of deviance would be a liability. Social-class homogeneity can be produced by building all homes of similar price, and life-style homogeneity can be encouraged through advertising campaigns designed to appeal to people with similar values and interests.

During the post-World War II period and beyond community planners in Britain and the United States drew on the community sociology literature and the ideas of visionaries, modern movement architects, and businessmen to design "garden cities" or "new towns" (Christensen, 1986; Lang, 1987). These projects were attempts to affect social life through design. Cooley's (1925) notion of the primary group, Park's (1925) idea that people should be rooted to a place to mediate against moral deviance, and the concerns about suburban life raised by Whyte (1956) and Reisman (1950) influenced planners (Christensen, 1986). Ebenezer Howard conceived of garden cities as towns designed for healthy living and industry, just large enough for a full measure of social life, with enough jobs to employ the residents, surrounded by a rural belt, with all of the land being publicly owned or held in trust for the community (Christensen, 1986). Modern movement architects (e.g., Le Corbusier, Clarence Perry, and Frank Lloyd Wright) believed that reducing the functional distance between households and the central placement of shopping, schools, and other community facilities would lead to the development of local friendships. Their goal was planning neighborhoods that were coterminous with a sense of community (Lang, 1987).

Both Britain and the United States undertook new town experiments, but neither was overwhelmingly successful (Corden, 1977). Examples of American new towns include Radburn, New Jersey, and Columbia, Maryland, (see Brooks, 1974; Christensen, 1986; Lang, 1987; and Stein, 1951 for detailed descriptions of these projects). In both Britain and the United States the amount of cooperation among individuals and among institutions was less than anticipated, and the desire for individual identity was much higher. This is congruent with the Western individualistic cultural context (Brooks, 1974). New town experiments convinced analysts that there are limitations to how successfully social ends can be achieved through physical design (Lang, 1987). Residents did not seem to respond to the physical environment in predicted ways. Although none of the analysts specifically addressed the issue of friendship patterns, their work implies that friendships were not significantly different than they would have been in a less planned community.

Among other causes, the failure of new town experiments to alter patterns of social interaction seems to have discouraged people from planning friendship interventions at the community level. Gans (1968) concluded that behavior is due more to the predispositions of residents than to the characteristics of the community. Smith (1979) attributed this decline of optimism about the possibility of changing social behavior through planning to the growth of social systems in size and complexity and the substitution of economic for social concerns. In either case, contemporary urban theory is much less utopian now than it was several decades ago.

We now know more about communities, planning, organizing, and friendship. We learned from the garden city and new town movement and from further research. We know, for example, that the ideal friendship patterns for individuals and social groups vary and that community plans must allow for diversity. More research is still needed, however, on the causes of difficulties in planned communities and possible solutions to such problems before it would be possible to recommend suitable designs for community-level friendship interventions.

Supporting Social Relationships
Through Social Policies

The societal level of analysis is the most remote from dyadic and network friendship interaction, and thus the least likely to be successful in enhancing friendship patterns. Moreover, policy analysts realize that government policies cannot cure all individual, relationship, and societal problems (Dye, 1981). A variety of reasons contributes to the limits of public policy, not the least of which is that social scientists do not know enough about individual and group behavior to provide reliable advice to policymakers (Dye, 1981). Nevertheless, we can find relevant evidence from the social science and family policy literatures to suggest potential interventions at the social policy level that might be successful in enhancing friendship patterns.

Family policy addresses the fundamental problems of families in relation to society (Zimmerman, 1988). Family policy may serve as an effective model for friendship intervention proposals because several theoretical frameworks for understanding family phenomena also apply to friendship. For example, the systems perspective, often used in family policy analysis, is relevant to friendship. Just as a family can be viewed as a social system, so, too, can a network of friends. The systems perspective emphasizes the transactional interdependence between families or friend networks and the government. Transactions are called *outputs* and *inputs* and refer to various kinds of resources, such as information, money, and people. Families and friend networks produce outputs as inputs for government, which, in turn, produces outputs as inputs for families and friend networks. Outputs in the form of government policies should contribute to stability of the immediate social environment so that families and friend networks can perform their tasks effectively. Policy strategies should be targeted to the environmental conditions of families and friend networks, not to direct interventions that invade family or friend network boundaries (Zimmerman, 1988).

An example of a policy area in which friend networks function extensively is provision of social services such as socialization for new roles and the maintenance of psychological well-being through social support. Friends might also contribute to physical health and many other domains of life. From the systems perspective a number of suggestions emerge about policies and programs to enhance supportive functions of friend networks. For example, policies that provide for respite programs enable caregivers of sick or frail relatives to socialize with their friends, maintaining the strength of friend ties and support. Another instance is Thompson and Heller's (1990) suggestion that policies designed to provide useful social roles for elderly citizens will benefit society through the tasks older persons perform, but will also benefit the elderly participants who will be perceived as interesting companions, thus increasing their chances of developing and maintaining friendships. As shown here, consideration of the reciprocal relationship between friends and society yields ideas for policies that could enhance friendship networks while benefiting other segments of society. Obviously, research is needed on whether or not the intended friendship outcome occurs with the advent of such policies.

❧ Implications

We do not necessarily intend to advocate friendship intervention. It is not yet clear whether such interventions are advisable or effective. As mentioned in the beginning of this chapter, interventions that affect friendship and other relationships occur all the time. Our point is that they should be responsibly designed; they should be grounded in sound research. Our theoretical model of friendship

(Chapter 1 and Figure 1.1) provides a framework for assessing whether knowledge is sufficiently advanced to devise various types and levels of responsible, potentially effective friendship interventions. We suggest that aging, other individual characteristics, social structure, culture, and history all affect the structure, processes, and phases of friendship patterns. Counselors, program planners, and policymakers need to consider the results of research on the structure and process of friendship patterns when developing plans for interventions that could affect social lives. For those interested in designing such interventions, we have suggested some applied literatures that might be of use.

Our model of friendship intervention (Figure 6.1) can be used in conjunction with the integrative model of friendship patterns (Chapter 1 and Figure 1.1) and the research findings reported in Chapters 3, 4, and 5 to develop intervention strategies and to think through their possible consequences. Interventions should sometimes be designed differently depending on the individual's stage of development, stage of the life course, psychological dispositions, and structural opportunities for and constraints on friendship. For example, the finding that sex-role orientation influences information processing about relationships (Chapter 4) suggests that persons attempting friendship-related cognitive interventions should attend to individuals' gender and personality characteristics as well as their cognitive processes. Although researchers have not often separated out the psychological and sociological effects on friendship patterns of age, gender, and other social and individual characteristics, the literature we reviewed in Chapters 3, 4, and 5 provides some bases for intervention designs that take these variations of experience into account. The scant findings about the interconnections among the various aspects of friendship patterns are also useful in designing interventions. The finding that dense friendship networks are higher in solidarity (Chapter 3), for example, suggests that one network-level intervention might be to introduce an individual's friends to one another. The research on the interconnections among the elements of friendship patterns is far from complete, however. In particular we need to know more about causality—which can only be understood by examining the results of longitudinal studies of relationships—and about the effects of context on friendship patterns. Only when these gaps in the literature have been filled will it be possible to plan friendship interventions safely and with confidence.

❧ Conclusions

Our model of friendship draws on the theoretical literatures of sociology and psychology and stems from recent trends in friendship research. We used this model to organize existing literature on friendship and to identify conceptual gaps and methodological limitations that should be addressed by future research. As new findings become available, the model should continue to be useful for assessing the state of theoretical and practical knowledge about this important type of social relationship.

The contributions of friendship to physical, social, and psychological well-being warrant continued and improved scholarly attention to study of this relationship. The early friendship researchers were pioneers, often conducting their studies in isolation from others with similar interests, relying on only a few publications for guidance. Now, as evidenced by our lengthy reference list, scholars are no longer hindered in this way. We believe that contemporary friendship researchers must conceptualize and conduct their studies with full awareness of how their endeavors correspond with those of others. Only then will the scattered threads of conceptual and empirical approaches to the analysis of friendship be tightly woven into a cloth that fully displays the color, texture, and pattern of the friend relationship.

References

Adams, R. G. (1983). *Friendship and its role in the lives of elderly women.* Unpublished doctoral dissertation, University of Chicago, Chicago, IL.

Adams, R. G. (1985). People would talk: Normative barriers to cross-sex friendship for elderly women. *The Gerontologist, 25,* 605-611.

Adams, R. G. (1985-86). Emotional closeness and physical distance between friends: Implications for elderly women living in age-segregated and age-integrated settings. *International Journal of Aging and Human Development, 22,* 55-75.

Adams, R. G. (1987). Patterns of network change: A longitudinal study of friendships of elderly women. *The Gerontologist, 27,* 222-227.

Adams, R. G. (1988, November). A gender-informed approach to friendship in late life. In T. M. Calasanti (Chair), *Incorporating gender into theory and research on aging.* Symposium presented at the 41st Annual Scientific Meeting of the Gerontological Society of America, San Francisco.

Adams, R. G. (1989). Conceptual and methodological issues in studying friendships of older adults. In R. G. Adams & R. Blieszner (Eds.), *Older adult friendship* (pp. 17-41). Newbury Park, CA: Sage.

Albert, S. M., & Moss, M. (1990). Consensus and the domain of personal relations among older adults. *Journal of Social and Personal Relationships, 7*, 353-369.

Allan, G. A. (1979). *A sociology of friendship and kinship.* London: George Allen & Unwin.

Allan, G. (1989). *Friendship.* New York: Harvester Wheatsheaf.

Allan, G., & Adams, R. G. (1989). Aging and the structure of friendship. In R. G. Adams & R. Blieszner (Eds.), *Older adult friendship* (pp. 45-64). Newbury Park, CA: Sage.

Altman, I., & Taylor, D. A. (1973). *Social penetration processes.* New York: Holt, Rinehart & Winston.

Antonucci, T. (1989). Understanding adult social relationships. In K. Kreppner & R. M. Lerner (Eds.), *Family systems and life-span development* (pp. 303-318). Hillsdale, NJ: Lawrence Erlbaum.

Argyle, M., & Furnham, A. (1983). Sources of satisfaction and conflict in long-term relationships. *Journal of Marriage and the Family, 45*, 481-493.

Argyle, M., & Henderson, M. (1984). The rules of friendship. *Journal of Social and Personal Relationships, 1*, 211-237.

Aries, E. J., & Johnson, F. L. (1983). Close friendship in adulthood: Conversational content between same-sex friends. *Sex Roles, 9*, 1183-1196.

Asher, S. R., & Gottman, J. M. (1981). Editorial preface. In S. R. Asher & J. M. Gottman (Eds.), *The development of children's friendships* (pp. xi-xiv). Cambridge, UK: Cambridge University Press.

Aukett, R., Ritchie, J., & Mill, K. (1988). Gender differences in friendship patterns. *Sex Roles, 19*, 57-66.

Ayres, J. (1983). Strategies to maintain relationships. *Communication Quarterly, 31*, 62-67.

Babbie, E. (1988). *The sociological spirit.* Belmont, CA: Wadsworth.

Babchuk, N., & Anderson, T. B. (1989). Older widows and married women: Their intimates and confidants. *International Journal of Aging and Human Development, 28*, 21-35.

Baker, P. M. (1983). The friendship process. *Sociological Spectrum, 3*, 265-279.

Baldassare, M. (1977). Residential density, household crowding, and social networks. In C. S. Fischer, R. M. Jackson, C. A. Stueve, K. Gerson, & L. M. Jones, with M. Baldassare, *Networks and places* (pp. 101-115). New York: Free Press.

Banikiotes, P. G., Neimeyer, G. J., & Lepkowsky, C. (1981). Gender and sex-role orientation effects on friendship choice. *Personality and Social Psychology Bulletin, 7*, 605-610.

Barker, R. G., & Wright, H. F. (1955). *The midwest and its children.* New York: Harper & Row.

Barnes, J. A. (1954). Class and committees in a Norwegian island parish. *Human Relations, 7*, 39-58.

Baron, R. S., Cutrona, C. E., Hicklin, D., Russell, D. W., & Lubaroff, D. M. (1990). Social support and immune function among spouses of cancer patients. *Journal of Personality and Social Psychology, 59,* 344-352.

Barth, R. J., & Kinder, B. N. (1988). A theoretical analysis of sex differences in same-sex friendships. *Sex Roles, 19,* 349-363.

Baxter, L. A. (1985). Accomplishing relationship disengagement. In S. Duck & D. Perlman (Eds.), *Understanding personal relationships* (pp. 243-265). London: Sage.

Baxter, L. A., & Wilmot, W. W. (1986). Interaction characteristics of disengaging, stable, and growing relationships. In R. Gilmour & S. Duck (Eds.), *The emerging field of personal relationships* (pp. 145-159). Hillsdale, NJ: Lawrence Erlbaum.

Bear, M. (1990). Social network characteristics and the duration of primary relationships after entry into long-term care. *Journal of Gerontology: Social Sciences, 45,* S156-162.

Becker, C. S. (1987). Friendship between women. *Journal of Phenomenological Psychology, 18,* 59-72.

Bell, R. R. (1981). *Worlds of friendship.* Beverly Hills: Sage.

Berg, J. H. (1984). Development of friendship between roommates. *Journal of Personality and Social Psychology, 46,* 346-356.

Berg, J. H., & Clark, M. S. (1986). Differences in social exchange between intimate and other relationships: Gradually evolving or quickly apparent? In V. J. Derlega & B. A. Winstead (Eds.), *Friendship and social interaction* (pp. 101-128). New York: Springer Verlag.

Berscheid, E. (1983). Emotion. In H. H. Kelley, E. Berscheid, A. Christensen, J. H. Harvey, T. L. Huston, G. Levinger, E. McClintock, L. A. Peplau, & D. R. Peterson, *Close relationships* (pp. 110-168). New York: Freeman.

Berscheid, E., Gangestad, S. W., & Kulakowski, D. (1984). Emotion in close relationships. In S. D. Brown & R. W. Lent (Eds.), *Handbook of counseling psychology* (pp.435-476). New York: John Wiley.

Biegel, D. E., Shore, B. K., & Gordon, E. (1984). *Building support networks for the elderly.* Beverly Hills: Sage.

Blackbird, T., & Wright, P. (1985). Pastors' friendships, part 1: Project overview and an exploration of the pedestal effect. *Journal of Psychology and Theology, 13,* 274-283.

Blankenship, V., Hnat, S. M., Hess, T. G., & Brown, D. R. (1984). Reciprocal interaction and similarity of personality attributes. *Journal of Social and Personal Relationships, 1,* 415-432.

Blau, Z. S. (1973). *Old age in a changing society.* New York: New Viewpoints.

Blieszner, R. (1982). Social relationships and life satisfaction in late adulthood. (Doctoral dissertation, The Pennsylvania State University, 1982). *Dissertation Abstracts International, 43,* 2366B. (University Microfilms No. 82-28863).

Blieszner, R. (1988). Individual development and intimate relationships in middle and late adulthood. In R. M. Milardo (Ed.), *Families and social networks* (pp. 147-167). Newbury Park, CA: Sage.

Blieszner, R. (1989a). An agenda for future research on friendships of older adults. In R. G. Adams & R. Blieszner (Eds.), *Older adult friendship* (pp. 245-252). Newbury Park, CA: Sage.

Blieszner, R. (1989b). Developmental processes of friendship. In R. G. Adams & R. Blieszner (Eds.), *Older adult friendship* (pp. 108-126). Newbury Park, CA: Sage.

Blieszner, R. (In press). Resource exchange in the social networks of elderly women. In U. G. Foa, J. M. Converse, & E. B. Foa (Eds.), *Resource theory*. San Diego, CA: Academic Press.

Bochner, S., Hutnik, N., & Furnham, A. (1985). The friendship patterns of overseas and host students in an Oxford student residence. *The Journal of Social Psychology, 125*, 689-694.

Bolotin, D. (1979). *Plato's dialogue on friendship*. Ithaca: Cornell University Press.

Booth, A., & Hess, E. (1974). Cross-sex friendship. *Journal of Marriage and the Family, 36*, 38-47.

Bossé, R., Aldwin, C. M., Levenson, M. R., Workman-Daniels, K., & Ekerdt, D. J. (1990). Differences in social support among retirees and workers. *Psychology and Aging, 5*, 41-47.

Bott, E. (1957). *Family and social network*. London: Tavistock.

Braiker, H. B., & Kelley, H. H. (1979). Conflict in the development of close relationships. In R. L. Burgess & T. L. Huston (Eds.), *Social exchange in developing relationships* (pp. 135-168). New York: Academic Press.

Brain, R. (1976). *Friends and lovers*. New York: Basic Books.

Bronfenbrenner, U. (1986). Ecology of the family as a context for human development. *Developmental Psychology, 22*, 723-742.

Brooks, R. O. (1974). *New towns and communal values*. New York: Praeger.

Brown, B. B. (1991). A life-span approach to friendship. In H. Z. Lopata & D. R. Maines (Eds.), *Friendship in context* (pp. 23-50). Greenwich, CT: JAI.

Brown, R. (1965). *Social psychology*. New York: Free Press.

Buhrke, R. A., & Fuqua, D. R. (1987). Sex differences in same- and cross-sex supportive relationships. *Sex Roles, 17*, 339-352.

Bukowski, W. M., Nappi, B. J., & Hoza, B. (1987). A test of Aristotle's model of friendship for young adults' same-sex and opposite-sex relationships. *The Journal of Social Psychology, 127*, 595-603.

Cahn, D. D. (1990). Perceived understanding and interpersonal relationships. *Journal of Social and Personal Relationships, 7*, 231-244.

Canary, D. J., & Cupach, W. R. (1988). Relational and episodic characteristics associated with conflict tactics. *Journal of Social and Personal Relationships, 5*, 305-325.

Candy, S. G., Troll, L. E., & Levy, S. G. (1981). A developmental exploration of friendship functions in women. *Psychology of Women Quarterly, 5,* 456-472.

Cate, R. M., & Lloyd, S. A. (1992). *Courtship.* Newbury Park, CA: Sage.

Cattell, R. B. (1934). Friends and enemies: A psychological study of character and temperament. *Character and Personality, 3,* 54-63.

Chown, S. M. (1981). Friendship in old age. In S. Duck & R. Gilmour (Eds.), *Personal relationships 2* (pp. 231-246). London: Academic Press.

Christensen, C. A. (1986). *The American Garden City and the New Towns Movement.* Ann Arbor, MI: UMI Research Press.

Clark, M. S. (1981). Noncomparability of benefits given and received: A cue to the existence of friendship. *Social Psychology Quarterly, 44,* 375-381.

Clark, M. S. (1984). Record keeping in two types of relationships. *Journal of Personality and Social Psychology, 47,* 549-557.

Clark, M. S., & Mills, J. (1979). Interpersonal attraction in exchange and communal relationships. *Journal of Personality and Social Psychology, 37,* 12-24.

Clark, M. S., Mills, J. R., & Corcoran, D. M. (1989). Keeping track of needs and inputs of friends and strangers. *Personality and Social Psychology Bulletin, 15,* 533-542.

Clark, M. S., & Reis, H. T. (1988). Interpersonal processes in close relationships. *Annual Review of Psychology, 39,* 609-672.

Cohen, C. I. (1989). Social ties and friendship patterns of old homeless men. In R. G. Adams & R. Blieszner (Eds.), *Older adult friendship* (pp. 222-242). Newbury Park, CA: Sage.

Cohen, C. I., & Rajkowski, H. (1982). What's in a friend? Substantive and theoretical issues. *The Gerontologist, 22,* 261-266.

Cohen, Y. A. (1961). *Social structure and personality.* New York: Holt, Rinehart & Winston.

Coleman, J. S. (1961). *The adolescent society.* New York: Free Press.

Coleman, S. B. (1977). A developmental stage hypothesis for non-marital dyadic relationships. *Journal of Marriage and Family Counseling, 3,* 71-76.

Connidis, I. A., & Davies, L. (1990). Confidants and companions in later life. *Journal of Gerontology: Social Sciences, 45,* S141-149.

Cooley, C. H. (1925). *Social organization.* New York: Scribner.

Corden, C. (1977). *Planned cities.* Beverly Hills: Sage.

Coser, L. (1977). *Masters of sociological thought.* New York: Harcourt Brace Jovanovich.

Cox, F. M., Erlich, J. L., Rothman, J., & Tropman, J. E. (1987). *Strategies of community organization.* Itasca, IL: F. E. Peacock.

Davidson, L. R., & Duberman, L. (1982). Friendship: Communication and interactional patterns in same-sex dyads. *Sex Roles, 8,* 809-822.

Derlega, V. J., Wilson, M., & Chaikin, A. L. (1976). Friendship and disclosure reciprocity. *Journal of Personality and Social Psychology, 34,* 578-582.

Dickson-Markman, F. (1986). Self-disclosure with friends across the life cycles. *Journal of Social and Personal Relationships, 3,* 259-264.

Duck, S. W. (1973). Personality similarity and friendship choice. *Journal of Personality, 41,* 543-558.

Duck, S. (1981). Toward a research map for the study of relationship breakdown. In S. Duck & R. Gilmour (Eds.), *Personal relationships 3* (pp. 1-29). London: Academic Press.

Duck, S. (1990). Relationships as unfinished business: Out of the frying pan and into the 1990s. *Journal of Social and Personal Relationships, 7,* 5-28.

Duck, S. W., & Craig, G. (1978). Personality similarity and the development of friendship. *British Journal of Social and Clinical Psychology, 17,* 237-242.

Duck, S., & Perlman, D. (1985). The thousand islands of personal relationships. In S. Duck & D. Perlman (Eds.), *Understanding personal relationships* (pp. 1-15). London: Sage.

Duck, S., Pond, K., & Leatham, G. (1991, May). *Remembering as a context for being in relationships.* Paper presented at the Third Conference of the International Network on Personal Relationships, Normal/Bloomington, IL.

Duck, S., Rutt, D. J., Hurst, M. H., & Strejc, H. (1991). Some evident truths about conversation in everyday relationships: All communications are not created equal. *Human Communication Research, 18,* 228-267.

Duck, S., & Sants, H. (1983). On the origin of the specious: Are personal relationships really interpersonal states? *Journal of Social and Clinical Psychology, 1,* 27-41.

Duck, S. W., & Spencer, C. P. (1972). Personal constructs and friendship formation. *Journal of Personality and Social Psychology, 23,* 40-45.

Dye, T. R. (1981). *Understanding family policy* (4th ed.). Englewood Cliffs, NJ: Prentice-Hall.

Dykstra, P. A. (1990). *Next of (non)kin.* Netherlands: Swets & Zeitlinger.

Elder, G. H., Jr., & Clipp, E. C. (1988). Wartime losses and social bonding. *Psychiatry, 51,* 177-198.

Epstein, N. (1981). Assertiveness training in marital treatment. In G. P. Sholevar (Ed.), *The handbook of marriage and marital therapy* (pp. 287-302). New York: Spectrum.

Erikson, E. H. (1950). *Childhood and society* (2nd ed.). New York: Norton.

Farrell, M. P., & Rosenberg, S. D. (1981). *Men at midlife.* Westport, CT: Auburn House.

Feger, H. (1981). Analysis of social networks. In S. Duck & R. Gilmour (Eds.), *Personal relationships 1* (pp. 91-108). London: Academic Press.

Feld, S. L. (1981). The focused organization of social ties. *American Journal of Sociology, 86,* 1015-1035.

Feld, S. L. (1982). Social structural determinants of similarity. *American Sociological Review, 45,* 797-801.

Feld, S. L., & Elmore, R. (1982). Patterns of sociometric choices. *Social Psychology Quarterly, 45,* 77-85.

Festinger, L., Schacter, S., & Back, K. (1950). *Social pressures in informal groups.* Palo Alto, CA: Stanford University Press.

Fischer, C. S. (1982). *To dwell among friends.* Chicago: University of Chicago Press.

Fischer, C. S., & Oliker, S. J. (1983). A research note on friendship, gender, and the life cycle. *Social Forces, 62,* 124-133.

Fischer, J. L., Sollie, D. L., Sorrell, G. T., & Green, S. K. (1989). Marital status and career stage influences on social networks of young adults. *Journal of Marriage and the Family, 51,* 521-534.

Fisher, C. B., Reid, J. D., & Melendez, M. (1989). Conflict in families and friendships of later life. *Family Relations, 38,* 83-89.

Fiske, M., & Chiriboga, D. A. (1990). *Change and continuity in adult life.* San Francisco: Jossey-Bass.

Flaschbart, P. G. (1969). Urban territorial behavior. *Journal of the American Institute of Planners, 25,* 412-416.

Fox, M., Gibbs, M., & Auerbach, D. (1985). Age and gender dimensions of friendship. *Psychology of Women Quarterly, 9,* 489-501.

Franck, K. A. (1980). Friends and strangers: The social experience of living in urban and non-urban settings. *Journal of Social Issues, 36*(3), 52-71.

Frank, O. (1981). A survey of statistical methods for graph analysis. In S. Leinhardt (Ed.), *Sociological methodology 1981* (pp. 110-155). San Francisco: Jossey-Bass.

Furnham, A., & Alibhai, N. (1985). The friendship networks of foreign students. *International Journal of Psychology, 20,* 709-722.

Gans, H. J. (1962). *The urban villagers.* Glencoe, IL: Free Press.

Gans, H. J. (1968). *People and plans.* New York: Basic Books.

Gans, H. J. (1976). Planning and social life: Friendship and neighbor relations in suburban communities. In H. Proshansky, W. H. Ittelson, & L. G. Rivlin (Eds.), *Environmental psychology* (pp. 564-573). New York: Holt, Rinehart & Winston.

Gerstel, N. (1988). Divorce, gender, and social integration. *Gender and Society, 2,* 343-367.

Gillespie, D. L., Krannich, R. S., & Leffler, A. (1985). The missing cell: Amiability, hostility, and gender differentiation in rural community networks. *The Social Science Journal, 22,* 17-30.

Goffman, E. (1971). *Relations in public.* New York: Basic Books.

Goldman, J. A., Cooper, P. E., Ahern, K., & Corsini, D. (1981). Continuities and discontinuities in the friendship descriptions of women at six stages in the life cycle. *Genetic Psychology Monographs, 103,* 153-167.

Goodman, C. C. (1985). Reciprocity among older adult peers. *Social Service Review, 59,* 269-282.

Gottlieb, B. H. (1988). Support interventions. In S. W. Duck (Ed.), *Handbook of personal relationships* (pp. 519-541). Chichester, England: John Wiley.

Gouldner, H., & Strong, M. S. (1987). *Speaking of friendship*. New York: Greenwood.

Griffin, E., & Sparks, G. G. (1990). Friends forever: A longitudinal exploration of intimacy in same-sex friends and platonic pairs. *Journal of Social and Personal Relationships, 7*, 29-46.

Guerney, B., Jr., Brock, G., & Coufal, J. (1986). Integrating marital therapy and enrichment. In N. S. Jacobson & A. S. Gurman (Eds.), *Clinical handbook of marital therapy* (pp. 151-172). New York: Guilford.

Gurman, A. S., & Kniskern, D. P. (1981). *Handbook of family therapy*. New York: Brunner/Mazel.

Hall, E. T. (1966). *The hidden dimension*. Garden City, NY: Doubleday.

Hall, E. T. (1989). *Understanding cultural differences*. Yarmouth, ME: Intercultural Press.

Hansson, R. O., Jones, W. H., & Fletcher, W. L. (1990). Troubled relationships in later life: Implications for support. *Journal of Social and Personal Relationships, 7*, 451-463.

Harrell, J., & Guerney, B. (1976). Training married couples in conflict negotiation skills. In D. H. L. Olson (Ed.), *Treating relationships* (pp. 151-165). Lake Mills, IA: Graphic.

Hays, R. B. (1984). The development and maintenance of friendship. *Journal of Social and Personal Relationships, 1*, 75-98.

Hays, R. B. (1985). A longitudinal study of friendship development. *Journal of Personality and Social Psychology, 48*, 909-924.

Hays, R. B. (1988). Friendship. In S. W. Duck (Ed.), *Handbook of personal relationships* (pp. 391-408). Chichester, England: Wiley.

Hays, R. B. (1989). The day-to-day functioning of close versus casual friendships. *Journal of Social and Personal Relationships, 6*, 21-37.

Healey, J. G., & Bell, R. A. (1990). Effects of social networks on individuals' responses to conflicts in friendship. In D. D. Cahn (Ed.), *Intimates in conflict* (pp. 121-150). Hillsdale, NJ: Lawrence Erlbaum.

Henderson, M., & Furnham, A. (1982a). Self-reported and self-attributed scores on personality, social skills, and attitudinal measures as compared between high and low nominated friends and acquaintances. *Psychological Reports, 50*, 88-90.

Henderson, M., & Furnham, A. (1982b). Similarity and attraction: The relationship between personality, beliefs, skills, needs and friendship choice. *Journal of Adolescence, 5*, 111-123.

Hendrick, S. S., & Hendrick, C. (1992). *Liking, loving, and relating* (2nd ed.). Pacific Grove, CA: Brooks/Cole.

Hess, B. B. (1972). Friendship. In M. W. Riley, M. Johnson, & A. Foner (Eds.), *Aging and society* (Vol. 3, pp. 357-393). New York: Russell Sage.

Hess, B. B. (1979). Sex roles, friendship, and the life course. *Research on Aging, 1,* 494-515.

Hill, C. T., & Stull, D. E. (1981). Sex differences in effects of social and value similarity in same-sex friendships. *Journal of Personality and Social Psychology, 41,* 488-502.

Hirsch, B. J. (1980). Psychological dimensions of social networks. *American Journal of Community Psychology, 7,* 263-278.

Hobfoll, S. E., & Stokes, J. P. (1988). The process and mechanics of social support. In S. W. Duck (Ed.), *Handbook of personal relationships* (pp. 497-517). Chichester, England: Wiley.

Hochschild, A. R. (1973). *The unexpected community.* Berkeley: University of California Press.

Ingersoll-Dayton, B., & Antonucci, T. C. (1988). Reciprocal and nonreciprocal social support. *Journal of Gerontology: Social Sciences, 43,* S65-73.

Jackson, R. M. (1977). Social structure and process in friendship choice. In C. S. Fischer, R. M. Jackson, C. A. Stueve, K. Gerson, & L. M. Jones, with M. Baldassare, *Networks and places* (pp. 59-78). New York: Free Press.

Jackson, R. M., Fischer, C. S., & Jones, L. C. (1977). The dimensions of social networks. In C. S. Fischer, R. M. Jackson, C. A. Stueve, K. Gerson, & L. M. Jones, with M. Baldassare, *Networks and places* (pp. 39-58). New York: Free Press.

Jacobson, D. (1968). Friendship and mobility in the development of an urban elite African social system. *Southwestern Journal of Anthropology, 24,* 123-138.

Johnsen, E. C. (1986). Structure and process: Agreement models for friendship formation. *Social Networks, 8,* 257-306.

Johnson, C. L. (1983). Fairweather friends and rainy day kin. *Urban Anthropology, 12,* 103-123.

Johnson, F. L., & Aries, E. J. (1983a). Conversational patterns among same-sex pairs of late-adolescent close friends. *The Journal of Genetic Psychology, 142,* 225-238.

Johnson, F. L., & Aries, E. J. (1983b). The talk of women friends. *Women's Studies International Forum, 6,* 353-361.

Johnson, M. A. (1989). Variables associated with friendship in an adult population. *The Journal of Social Psychology, 129,* 379-390.

Johnson, M. P., & Leslie, L. (1982). Couple involvement and network structure: A test of the dyadic withdrawal hypothesis. *Social Psychology Quarterly, 45,* 34-43.

Jones, D. C. (1991). Friendship satisfaction and gender. *Journal of Social and Personal Relationships, 8,* 167-185.

Jones, D. C., & Vaughan, K. (1990). Close friendships among senior adults. *Psychology and Aging, 5,* 451-457.

Kapferer, B. (1969). Norms and the manipulation of relationships in a work context. In J. C. Mitchell (Ed.), *Social networks in urban situations* (pp. 181-244). Manchester, England: Manchester University Press.

Keller, S. I. (1968). *The urban neighborhood.* New York: Random House.

Kelley, H. H., Berscheid, E., Christensen, A., Harvey, J. H., Huston, T. L., Levinger, G., McClintock, E., Peplau, L. A., & Peterson, D. R. (1983). Analyzing close relationships. In H. H. Kelley et al., *Close relationships* (pp. 20-67). New York: Freeman.

Kephart, W. M. (1950). A quantitative analysis of intergroup relationships. *American Journal of Sociology, 54,* 544-549.

Kernis, M. H., & Wheeler, L. (1981). Beautiful friends and ugly strangers: Radiation and contrast effects in perceptions of same-sex pairs. *Personality and Social Psychology Bulletin, 7,* 617-620.

Kerr, M. E., & Bowen, M. (1988). *Family evaluation.* New York: Norton.

Kimmel, D. C. (1979). Relationship initiation and development: A life-span developmental approach. In R. L. Burgess & T. L. Huston (Eds.), *Social exchange in developing relationships* (pp. 351-377). New York: Academic Press.

Knapp, C. W., & Harwood, B. T. (1977). Factors in the determination of intimate same-sex friendship. *The Journal of Genetic Psychology, 131,* 83-90.

Kogan, N. (1990). Personality and aging. In J. E. Birren & K. W. Schaie (Eds.), *Handbook of the psychology of aging* (3rd ed., pp. 330-346). San Diego: Academic Press.

LaBranche, A. (1975-76). My friendships—and personal freedom. *Review of Existential Psychology and Psychiatry, 14,* 81-85.

LaGaipa, J. J. (1977). Testing a multidimensional approach to friendship. In S. Duck (Ed.), *Theory and practice in interpersonal attraction* (pp. 249-270). London: Academic Press.

Lang, J. (1987). *Creating architectural theory.* New York: Van Nostrand Reinhold.

Larson, R. (1978). Thirty years of research on the subjective well-being of older Americans. *Journal of Gerontology, 33,* 109-125.

Laumann, E. O. (1973). *Bonds of pluralism.* New York: John Wiley.

Lawton, M. P. (1975). *Planning and managing housing for the elderly.* New York: John Wiley.

Lea, M., & Duck, S. (1982). A model for the role of similarity of values in friendship development. *British Journal of Social Psychology, 21,* 301-310.

Levinger, G., & Snoek, J. D. (1972). *Attraction in relationship: A new look at interpersonal attraction.* Morristown, NJ: General Learning Press.

Liebow, E. (1967). *Tally's corner.* Boston: Little, Brown.

Litwak, E. (1989). Forms of friendships among older people in an industrial society. In R. G. Adams & R. Blieszner (Eds.), *Older adult friendship* (pp. 65-88). Newbury Park, CA: Sage.

Litwak, E., & Szelenyi, I. (1969). Primary group structures and their functions. *American Sociological Review, 34,* 465-481.

Lopata, H. Z. (1979). *Women as widows.* New York: Elsevier North-Holland.

Lopata, H. Z. (1991). Friendship: Historical and theoretical introduction. In H. Z. Lopata & D. R. Maines (Eds.), *Friendship in context* (pp. 1-22). Greenwich, CT: JAI.

Lowy, L. (1985). *Social work with the aging.* New York: Longman.

Malloy, T. E., & Albright, L. (1990). Interpersonal perception in a social context. *Journal of Personality and Social Psychology, 58,* 419-428.

Mancini, J. A., & Blieszner, R. (1992). Social provisions in adulthood. *Journal of Gerontology: Psychological Sciences, 47,* P14-20.

Marsden, P., & Campbell, K. (1984). Measuring tie strength. *Social Forces, 63,* 482-501.

Matthews, S. H. (1983). Definitions of friendship and their consequences in old age. *Ageing and Society, 3,* 141-155.

Matthews, S. H. (1986). *Friendships through the life course.* Beverly Hills: Sage.

McCall, G. J. (1988). The organizational life cycle of relationships. In S. W. Duck (Ed.), *Handbook of personal relationships* (pp. 467-484). Chichester, England: John Wiley.

McCarthy, B., & Duck, S. W. (1976). Friendship duration and responses to attitudinal agreement-disagreement. *British Journal of Clinical and Social Psychology, 15,* 377-386.

McPherson, J. M., & Smith-Lovin, L. (1987). Homophily in voluntary organizations. *American Sociological Review, 52,* 370-379.

McWilliams, S., & Blumstein, P. (1991). Evaluative hierarchies in personal relationships. In E. Lawler, B. Markovsky, C. Ridgeway, & H. Walker (Eds.), *Advances in group processes* (Vol. 8, pp. 67-88). Greenwich, CT: JAI.

Miell, D., & Duck, S. (1986). Strategies in developing friendships. In V. J. Derlega & B. A. Winstead (Eds.), *Friendship and social interaction* (pp. 129-143). New York: Springer Verlag.

Milardo, R. M. (1982). Friendship networks in developing relationships. *Social Psychology Quarterly, 45,* 162-172.

Mitchell, J. C. (1969). The concept and use of social networks. In J. C. Mitchell (Ed.), *Social networks in urban situations* (pp. 1-50). Manchester, England: Manchester University Press.

Mogey, J. M. (1956). *Family and neighborhood.* London: Oxford University Press.

Moreno, J. L. (1934). *Who shall survive?* Washington, DC: Nervous and Mental Disease Publishing.

Morse, S. J., & Marks, A. (1985). " 'Cause Duncan's me mate": A comparison of reported relations with mates and with friends in Australia. *British Journal of Social Psychology, 24,* 283-292.

Murstein, B. I., & Spitz, L. T. (1973-74). Aristotle and friendship. *Interpersonal Development, 4,* 21-34.

Nahemow, L., & Lawton, M. P. (1975). Similarity and propinquity in friendship formation. *Journal of Personality and Social Psychology, 32,* 205-213.

Neimeyer, G. J., & Neimeyer, R. A. (1985). Relational trajectories. *Journal of Social and Personal Relationships, 2,* 325-349.

Neimeyer, G. J., & Neimeyer, R. A. (1986). Personal constructs in relationship deterioration. *Social Behavior and Personality, 14,* 253-257.

Neimeyer, R. A., & Mitchell, K. A. (1988). Similarity and attraction. *Journal of Social and Personal Relationships, 5,* 131-148.

Neugarten, B. L., & Hagestad, G. O. (1985). Age and the life course. In R. H. Binstock & E. Shanas (Eds.), *Handbook of aging and the social sciences* (pp. 35-61). New York: Van Nostrand Reinhold.

Neugarten, B. L., & Neugarten, D. A. (1986). Age in the aging society. *Daedalus, 115,* 31-50.

Newcomb, T. M. (1961). *The acquaintance process.* New York: Holt, Rinehart & Winston.

Niemeijer, R. (1973). Some applications of the notion of density. In J. Boissevain & J. C. Mitchell (Eds.), *Network analyses* (pp. 45-67). The Hague: Mouton.

O'Connell, L. (1984). An exploration of exchange in three social relationships: Kinship, friendship and the marketplace. *Journal of Social and Personal Relationships, 1,* 333-345.

O'Keefe, D. J. (1990). *Persuasion.* Newbury Park, CA: Sage.

Oliker, S. J. (1989). *Best friends and marriage.* Berkeley, CA: University of California Press.

Osmond, H. (1966). Some psychiatric aspects of design. In L. B. Holland (Ed.), *Who designs America?* (pp. 281-318). New York: Doubleday.

Paine, R. (1969). In search of friendship: An exploratory analysis in "Middle-class" culture. *Man, 4,* 505-524.

Pakaluck, M. (1991). *Other selves: Philosophers on friendship.* Indianapolis, IN: Hackett.

Parish, W. L. (1973). Internal migration and modernization: The European case. *Economic Development and Cultural Change, 21,* 591-609.

Park, R. E. (1925). *The city.* Chicago: University of Chicago Press.

Peplau, L. A., & Perlman, D. (Eds.). (1982). *Loneliness.* New York: John Wiley-Interscience.

Peretti, P. O. (1976). Closest friendships of black college students: Social intimacy. *Adolescence, 11,* 395-403.

Peretti, P. O. (1977). Closest friendships of black college students: Structural characteristics. *Human Relations, 30,* 43-51.

Peterson, G. W., & Rollins, B. C. (1987). Parent-child socialization. In M. B. Sussman & S. K. Steinmetz (Eds.), *Handbook of marriage and the family* (pp. 471-507). New York: Plenum.

Pihlblad, C. T., & Adams, D. L. (1972). Widowhood, social participation and life satisfaction. *Aging and Human Development, 3,* 323-330.

Piker, S. (1968). Friendship to the death in rural Thai society. *Human Organization, 27,* 200-204.

Price, A. W. (1989). *Love and friendship in Plato and Aristotle.* Oxford: Clarendon.

Raiffa, H. (1982). *The art and science of negotiation.* Cambridge, MA: Harvard University Press.

Rands, M., & Levinger, G. (1979). Implicit theories of relationship. *Journal of Personality and Social Psychology, 37,* 645-661.

Rawlins, W. K. (1983a). Negotiating close friendship. *Human Communication Research, 9,* 255-266.

Rawlins, W. K. (1983b). Openness as a problematic in ongoing friendships. *Communication Monographs, 50,* 1-13.

Reisman, D. (1950). *The lonely crowd.* New Haven, CT: Yale University Press.

Reisman, J. M. (1981). Adult friendships. In S. Duck & R. Gilmour (Eds.), *Personal relationships 2* (pp. 205-230). London: Academic Press.

Reisman, J. M. (1990). Intimacy in same-sex friendships. *Sex Roles, 23,* 65-82.

Reisman, J. M., & Shorr, S. I. (1978). Friendship claims and expectations among children and adults. *Child Development, 49,* 913-916.

Renshaw, P. D. (1981). The roots of peer interaction research: A historical analysis of the 1930s. In S. R. Asher & J. M. Gottman (Eds.), *The development of children's friendships* (pp. 1-25). Cambridge, UK: Cambridge University Press.

Retsinas, J., & Garrity, P. (1985). Nursing home friendships. *The Gerontologist, 25,* 376-381.

Richardson, V. (1984). Clinical-historical aspects of friendship deprivation among women. *Social Work Research and Abstracts, 20,* 19-24.

Roberto, K. A. (1989). Exchange and equity in friendships. In R. G. Adams & R. Blieszner (Eds.), *Older adult friendship* (pp. 147-165). Newbury Park, CA: Sage.

Roberto, K. A., & Scott, J. P. (1984-85). Friendship patterns among older women. *International Journal of Aging and Human Development, 19,* 1-10.

Roberto, K. A., & Scott, J. P. (1986a). Equity considerations in the friendships of older adults. *Journal of Gerontology, 41,* 241-247.

Roberto, K. A., & Scott, J. P. (1986b). Friendships of older men and women: Exchange patterns and satisfaction. *Psychology and Aging, 1,* 103-109.

Rodin, M. J. (1978). Liking and disliking. *Personality and Social Psychology Bulletin, 4,* 473-478.

Rook, K. S. (1984). Promoting social bonding. *American Psychologist, 39,* 1389-1407.

Rook, K. S. (1987). Reciprocity of social exchange and social satisfaction among older women. *Journal of Personality and Social Psychology, 52,* 145-154.

Rook, K. S. (1989). Strains in older adults' friendships. In R. G. Adams & R. Blieszner (Eds.), *Older adult friendship* (pp. 166-194). Newbury Park, CA: Sage.

Rose, S. M. (1984). How friendships end. *Journal of Social and Personal Relationships, 1,* 267-277.

Rose, S. M. (1985). Same- and cross-sex friendships and the psychology of homosociality. *Sex Roles, 12,* 63-74.

Rose, S., & Roades, L. (1987). Feminism and women's friendships. *Psychology of Women Quarterly, 11,* 243-254.

Rose, S., & Serafica, F. C. (1986). Keeping and ending close and best friendships. *Journal of Social and Personal Relationships, 3,* 275-288.

Rosow, I. (1967). *Social integration of the aged.* New York: Free Press.

Rubin, K. H., & Ross, H. S. (1982). Some reflections on the state of the art: The study of peer relationships and social skills. In K. H. Rubin & H. S. Ross (Eds.), *Peer relationships and social skills in childhood* (pp. 1-8). New York: Springer Verlag.

Rubin, L. B. (1985). *Just friends.* New York: Harper & Row.

Rueveni, U. (1979). *Networking families in crisis.* New York: Human Sciences Press.

Rusbult, C. E. (1987). Responses to dissatisfaction in close relationships. In D. Perlman & S. Duck (Eds.), *Intimate relationships* (pp. 209-237). Newbury Park, CA: Sage.

Rushton, J. (1989). Genetic similarity in male friendships. *Ethology and Sociobiology, 10,* 361-373.

Sahakian, W. S. (1974). *Systematic social psychology.* New York: Chandler.

Salzinger, L. L. (1982). The ties that bind: The effect of clustering on dyadic relationships. *Social Networks, 4,* 117-145.

Schutte, J. G., & Light, J. M. (1978). The relative importance of proximity and status for friendship choices in social hierarchies. *Social Psychology, 41,* 260-264.

Seeley, J. R., Sim, R. A., & Loosley, E. W. (1956). *Crestwood Heights.* New York: John Wiley.

Selman, R. (1981). The child as friendship philosopher. In S. R. Asher & J. M. Gottman (Eds.), *The development of children's friendships* (pp. 242-272). Cambridge, UK: Cambridge University Press.

Shapiro, E. G. (1980). Is seeking help from a friend like seeking help from a stranger? *Social Psychology Quarterly, 43,* 259-263.

Shea, L., Thompson, L., & Blieszner, R. (1988). Resources in older adults' old and new friendships. *Journal of Social and Personal Relationships, 5,* 83-96.

Silver, A. (1990). Friendship in commercial society: Eighteenth-century social theory and modern sociology. *American Journal of Sociology, 95,* 1474-1504.

Simmel, G. (1955). *The web of group affiliations* (R. Bendix, Trans.). Glencoe, IL: Free Press. (Original work published 1922)

Smith, M. P. (1979). *The city and social theory*. New York: St. Martin's.

Smith-Rosenberg, C. (1975). The female world of love and ritual: Relations between women in nineteenth-century America. *Signs, 1*, 1-29.

Smollar, J., & Youniss, J. (1982). Social development through friendship. In K. H. Rubin & H. S. Ross (Eds.), *Peer relationships and social skills in childhood* (pp. 279-298). New York: Springer Verlag.

Snell, W. E., Jr. (1989). Willingness to self-disclose to female and male friends as a function of social anxiety and gender. *Personality and Social Psychology Bulletin, 15*, 113-125.

Snyder, M., Gangestad, S., & Simpson, J. A. (1983). Choosing friends as activity partners: The role of self-monitoring. *Journal of Personality and Social Psychology, 45*, 1061-1072.

Snyder, M., & Smith, D. (1986). Personality and friendship: The friendship worlds of self-monitoring. In V. J. Derlega & B. A. Winstead (Eds.), *Friendship and social interaction* (pp. 63-80). New York: Springer Verlag.

Sommer, R. (1969). *Personal space*. Englewood Cliffs, NJ: Prentice-Hall.

Spakes, P. R. (1979). Family, friendship and community interaction as related to life satisfaction of the elderly. *Journal of Gerontological Social Work, 1*, 279-293.

Stein, C. (1951). *Towards new towns for America*. Chicago: Public Administration Service.

Stein, P. J. (1986). Men and their friendships. In R. A. Lewis & R. E. Salt (Eds.), *Men in families* (pp. 261-269). Beverly Hills, CA: Sage.

Stueve, C. A., & Gerson, K. (1977). Personal relations across the life-cycle. In C. S. Fischer, R. M. Jackson, C. A. Stueve, K. Gerson, & L. M. Jones, with M. Baldassare, *Networks and places* (pp. 79-98). New York: Free Press.

Suitor, J. J. (1987). Friendship networks in transition. *Journal of Social and Personal Relationships, 4*, 445-461.

Sutcliffe, J. P., & Crabbe, B. D. (1963). Incidence and degrees of friendship in urban and rural areas. *Social Forces, 42*, 60-67.

Suttles, G. D. (1970). Friendship as a social institution. In G. McCall, M. M. McCall, N. K. Denzin, G. D. Suttles, & S. B. Kurth, *Social relationships* (pp. 95-135). Chicago: Aldine.

Swain, S. (1989). Covert intimacy: Closeness in men's friendships. In B. J. Risman & P. Schwartz (Eds.), *Gender in intimate relationships* (pp. 71-86). Belmont, CA: Wadsworth.

Tesch, S. A. (1989). Early-life development and adult friendship. In R. G. Adams & R. Blieszner (Eds.), *Older adult friendship* (pp.89-107). Newbury Park, CA: Sage.

Tesch, S. A., & Martin, R. R. (1983). Friendship concepts of young adults in two age groups. *Journal of Psychology, 115*, 7-12.

Thomas, L. (1987). Friendship. *Synthese, 72*, 217-236.

Thompson, M. G., & Heller, K. (1990). Facets of support related to well-being. *Psychology and Aging, 5,* 535-544.

Ting-Toomey, S. (1981). Ethnic identity and close friendship in Chinese-American college students. *International Journal of Intercultural Relations, 5,* 383-406.

Tognoli, J. (1980). Male friendship and intimacy across the life span. *Family Relations, 29,* 273-279.

Tokuno, K. A. (1986). The early adult transition and friendships: Mechanisms of support. *Adolescence, 21,* 593-606.

Tonnies, F. (1940). *Fundamental concepts of sociology* (C. P. Loomis, Trans.) New York: American Book Company. (Original work published 1887)

Törnblom, K. Y., & Fredholm, E. M. (1984). Attribution of friendship: The influence of the nature and comparability of resources given and received. *Social Psychology Quarterly, 47,* 50-61.

Törnblom, K. Y., Fredholm, E. M., & Jonsson, D. R. (1987). New and old friendships: Attributed effects of type and similarity of transacted resources. *Human Relations, 40,* 337-360.

Trower, P. (1981). Social skill disorder. In S. Duck & R. Gilmour (Eds.), *Personal relationships 3* (pp. 97-110). London: Academic Press.

Tschann, J. M. (1988). Self-disclosure in adult friendship: Gender and marital status differences. *Journal of Social and Personal Relationships, 5,* 65-81.

Usui, W. M. (1984). Homogeneity of friendship networks of elderly blacks and whites. *Journal of Gerontology, 39,* 350-356.

VanLear, C. A., & Trujillo, N. (1986). On becoming acquainted: A longitudinal study of social judgement processes. *Journal of Social and Personal Relationships, 3,* 375-392.

Verbrugge, L. M. (1977). The structure of adult friendship choices. *Social Forces, 56,* 576-597.

Verbrugge, L. M. (1983). A research note on adult friendship contact: A dyadic perspective. *Social Forces, 62,* 78-83.

Wall, S. M., Pickert, S. M., & Paradise, L. V. (1984). American men's friendships. *The Journal of Psychology, 116,* 179-186.

Webber, M. (1970). Order in diversity: Community without propinquity. In R. Gutman & D. Popenoe (Eds.), *Neighborhood, city, and metropolis* (pp. 791-811). New York: Random House.

Weber, M. (1947). *The theory of social and economic organization.* New York: Free Press.

Weiss, L., & Lowenthal, M. F. (1975). Life-course perspectives on friendship. In M. E. Lowenthal, M. Thurnher, D. Chiriboga, & Associates, *Four stages of life* (pp. 48-61). San Francisco: Jossey-Bass.

Weiss, R. S. (1973). *Loneliness.* Cambridge: MIT Press.

Wellman, B. (1983). Network analysis. In R. Collins (Ed.), *Sociological theory* (pp. 155-200). San Francisco: Jossey-Bass.

Wellman, B. (1988). Structural analysis. In B. Wellman & S. D. Berkowitz (Eds.), *Social structures* (pp. 19-61). New York: Cambridge University Press.

Werner, C., & Parmelee, P. (1979). Similarity of activity preferences among friends. *Social Psychology Quarterly, 42,* 62-66.

Westin, A. (1970). *Privacy and freedom.* New York: Ballantine.

Whyte, W. H. (1956). *The organization man.* New York: Simon & Schuster.

Wicker, A. W. (1979). *An introduction to ecological psychology.* Monterey, CA: Brooks/Cole.

Williams, D. G. (1985). Gender, masculinity-femininity, and emotional intimacy in same-sex friendship. *Sex Roles, 12,* 587-600.

Williams, R. (1959). Friendship and social values in a suburban community. *Pacific Sociological Review, 2,* 3-10.

Winkler, J. (1981). *Bargaining for results.* London: Heinemann.

Wiseman, J. P. (1986). Friendship: Bonds and binds in a voluntary relationship. *Journal of Social and Personal Relationships, 3,* 191-211.

Wister, A. V., & Avison, W. R. (1982). "Friendly persuasion": A social network analysis of sex differences in marijuana use. *The International Journal of the Addictions, 17,* 523-541.

Wolff, K. H. (Ed. & Trans.). (1950). *The sociology of Georg Simmel.* New York: Free Press.

Won-Doornink, M. J. (1985). Self-disclosure and reciprocity in conversation. *Social Psychology Quarterly, 48,* 97-107.

Wright, P. H. (1982). Men's friendships, women's friendships, and the alleged inferiority of the latter. *Sex Roles, 8,* 1-20.

Wright, P. H. (1984). Self-referent motivation and the intrinsic quality of friendship. *Journal of Social and Personal Relationships, 1,* 115-130.

Wright, P. H. (1989). Gender differences in adults' same- and cross-gender friendships. In R. G. Adams & R. Blieszner (Eds.), *Older adult friendship* (pp. 197-221). Newbury Park, CA: Sage.

Wright, P. H., & Blackbird, T. (1986). Pastors' friendships, part 2: The impact of congregational norms. *Journal of Psychology and Theology, 14,* 29-41.

Yancy, W. L. (1976). Architecture, interaction, and social control. In H. Proshansky, W. H. Ittelson, & L. G. Rivlin (Eds.), *Environmental psychology* (pp. 449-458). New York: Holt, Rinehart & Winston.

Young, J. E. (1986). A cognitive-behavioral approach to friendship disorders. In V. J. Derlega & B. A. Winstead (Eds.), *Friendship and social interaction* (pp. 247-276). New York: Springer Verlag.

Zimmerman, S. L. (1988). *Understanding family policy.* Newbury Park, CA: Sage.

Index

Acquaintances, 15, 34, 64-65, 67, 70, 80, 84, 93, 105
Acquaintanceship, 17, 36, 83, 90, 92, 106
Adolescent friendship, 33
Adult friendship, 47-51, 62, 74-79, 96-98; compared to college student friendships, 47-48; problems with studies of, 47. *See also* Middle-age friendship
Affective processes, 13, 15, 18, 61, 88-89; anxiety, 113; commitment, 37, 62, 85-97; competitiveness, 97; concern, 62; disliking, 67; effects of gender on, 67-68, 75; effects of size on, 81; emotion management, 75-76; enjoyment, 81; fear of closeness, 97; lack of studies across genders and stages of the life course, 86; liking, 66-69; predictors of, 67, 80; respect, 62; satisfaction, 13, 68,

71, 75, 80-81, 94-95, 108, 111-112; trust, 13, 62, 68, 71, 83, 75, 85, 91-92, 97, 111
Age. *See* Social and individual characteristics
Age density, 115

Behavioral processes, 13, 18, 61, 88-89, 108-109; activities, 62, 65, 69, 76, 80, 84, 94; affection, 6, 68-69, 80, 82, 86-87, 92, 94-95, 101-102, 111; betrayal, 83-84; companionship, 82, 85; communication, 35-36, 69-70, 76-77, 82, 87, 92, 95, 97, 101-102; conflict, 14, 37, 71, 77, 81-83, 94; conflict strategies, 71, 112-113; effects of cultural context on, 69-70; effects of friendship phases on, 82-83, 87;

141

About the Authors

Rosemary Blieszner is Associate Professor in the Department of Family and Child Development and Associate Director of the Center for Gerontology at Virginia Polytechnic Institute and State University. She received the Ph.D. from The Pennsylvania State University in Human Development—Family Studies with a concentration in Adult Development and Aging. Her research focuses on family and friend relationships and life events in adulthood and old age. Currently she is examining the contributions of close relationships between friends and between adult children and aging parents to personal development and psychological well-being.

Rebecca G. Adams is Associate Professor in the Department of Sociology at the University of North Carolina at Greensboro. She received the Ph.D. from the University of Chicago, with an emphasis on the Sociology of Aging. Her major research interest is friendship patterns, especially as they are affected by geographic separation and by cultural and structural context. Currently she is examining the cultural conventions and structural conditions affecting the development of friendships among members of a nonterritorial music subculture.

Dr. Adams and Dr. Blieszner co-edited *Older Adult Friendship: Structure and Process* (Sage, 1989). They are collaborating on a study of older adult friendship patterns and their effects on mental health. They plan to continue working together on research related to the conceptual model of friendship presented in this volume.